Thomas Jefferson Morgan

The Negro in America, and the Ideal American Republic

Thomas Jefferson Morgan

The Negro in America, and the Ideal American Republic

ISBN/EAN: 9783337022662

Printed in Europe, USA, Canada, Australia, Japan

Cover: Foto ©Suzi / pixelio.de

More available books at **www.hansebooks.com**

The Negro in America

And

The Ideal American Republic

BY

T. J. MORGAN, D. D., LL. D.

AUTHOR OF

"*Studies in Pedagogy*," "*Patriotic Citizenship*," *etc.*

PHILADELPHIA
AMERICAN BAPTIST PUBLICATION SOCIETY
1420 Chestnut Street

Copyright 1898 by the
AMERICAN BAPTIST PUBLICATION SOCIETY

From the Society's own Press

Dedicated

TO THE OFFICERS AND SOLDIERS WHOM I HAD THE HONOR TO COMMAND DURING THE WAR FOR THE ENLARGEMENT OF HUMAN LIBERTY, THE PERPETUATION OF FREE INSTITUTIONS, AND THE PRESERVATION OF THE REPUBLIC—"A GOVERNMENT OF THE PEOPLE, BY THE PEOPLE, AND FOR THE PEOPLE"

PREFATORY NOTE

My grandfather was a slaveholder. My father was an Abolitionist. While a student in college I learned to believe in the doctrine of the brotherhood of man and to hate slavery. During the war I organized four regiments of Negro soldiers; was colonel of the Fourteenth U. S. Colored Infantry; organized and commanded the First Colored Brigade of the Army of the Cumberland, and participated in numerous engagements with both white and black soldiers. Since the war I have had an abiding and growing interest in the progress of the Negroes. For more than five years, as the executive officer of the American Baptist Home Mission Society, under whose auspices an extensive educational and missionary work has been carried on for the Negroes, I have had occasion to study their conditions critically, to make frequent public addresses, and to write numerous essays. Some of these are

Prefatory Note

now printed together with the hope that they may be serviceable as well as interesting. Written at different times, for specific purposes, with no intention of making a book, the essays contain a little repetition and lack of unity, defects which I hope the reader will kindly pardon. I could not remedy them without marring the individuality of the papers.

The essay on "The Ideal Republic" is added because it sets forth the essential principles underlying the relation of eight million Negroes to their fellow-citizens of the republic. The final solution of this great question holds in it very much for weal or woe not only for the Negroes and their descendants, but also for all that mighty host who are to constitute the Twentieth Century Republic.

T. J. M.

NEW YORK, November, 1898.

CONTENTS

		PAGE
I.	SLAVERY AND FREEDOM	9
II.	NEGROES IN THE CIVIL WAR	52
III.	EDUCATION OF THE NEGROES	75
IV.	THE HIGHER EDUCATION OF NEGRO WOMEN	96
V.	RELIGIOUS LIFE AMONG THE NEGROES	115
VI.	NEGROPHOBIA	123
VII.	THE NEGROES UNDER FREEDOM	143
VIII.	THE IDEAL AMERICAN REPUBLIC	160

THE NEGRO IN AMERICA

I

SLAVERY AND FREEDOM

The population of the United States now comprises probably seventy millions of people, and among these are representatives of all the great races of the earth. About four hundred years ago, when adventurers from Europe came to explore North America they found living here a body of copper-colored people whom they called Indians. Where these people came from, how they got here, why they came, or how many there were of them, nobody knows. In the early part of the seventeenth century colonists arriving from Europe began to form settlements along the Atlantic coast, and European immigrants have continued to come until the number has reached the enormous proportion of about twenty millions. Almost all of these people came of their own free will, to establish for themselves homes in

The Negro in America

a new country, where the conditions would be more favorable for their prosperity and happiness than in the lands from which they came. They and their descendants constitute by far the largest part of our population, and they have been the chief factors in the development of our civilization.

The "Mayflower" and the Slave Ship

The Africans brought to this country were not immigrants, coming of their own free will to seek their fortunes in a new country; they were captives, seized in Africa, carried away from their native land, their homes, their friends, and brought to this country in the holds of sailing vessels where they suffered many hardships, and were sold into slavery. The first slave-ship landed at Jamestown, Va., 1619, with its helpless cargo, and thus introduced on American soil an institution which was destined to play a very significant part in the future history of the American people. The "Mayflower," which landed at Plymouth, Mass., in 1620, brought a company of intelligent Christian white people, who laid the foundations of a new civilization characterized by freedom : out of the Plymouth Colony have come free schools, free Bibles, free ballots. America is pre-eminently the land of equality. Every citizen of the republic has the right to life, liberty, and the pursuit of happiness, and rightfully claims the equal protection of the laws under which he lives. The slave-ship brought slaves, those who could claim no rights whatever, but were to receive in silence and submission whatever treatment was accorded to them by their masters. In a new country such as this then was, there was great need of labor; and the slave trade was very profitable, because there was great demand for the work of the poor creatures who were brought from Africa to America.

At first the Africans were sold to any who would buy them in any of the Colonies; slavery existed in the Northern portions of the country as well as in the Southern. In the course of time, however, slavery came to be confined entirely to the Southern States. The Northern communities abandoned it partly because it was less profitable in the North and partly because of the growth of a strong public sentiment against it.

Slaves were used for the performance of all kinds of service: the women as cooks, chambermaids, laundresses, sewing girls, nurses; the men as coachmen, gardeners, field hands. A very large part of the hardest work in the South was done by the slaves, and those who could afford to do so usually preferred to own their servants rather than to hire them, as was generally done at the North, and is now done everywhere in the country. Many slaveholders were kind-hearted, noble, worthy people, who either did not see anything wrong in slavery, or who, because they had inherited their slaves, or for other reasons which seemed to them sufficient, could not very well divest themselves of slave property.

In very many instances the slaves were kindly treated, being fairly well clothed and fed, and properly cared for when sick; in other cases they were treated very harshly and even cruelly. They were not taught to read or write; they did not own property; everything they had belonged to their masters; they were not allowed to have their own homes, but must live wherever required to by their masters; sometimes a husband lived on one plantation and his wife on another, while the children, perhaps, were sold and carried away into distant States. Slavery left no place for

Slavery and Freedom

the recognition of manhood and womanhood; it made no provision for the cultivation of self-respect, industry, thrift, intelligence, enterprise, independence; it crushed out in the slave most of the nobler sentiments of the human heart. Slavery was a monster, and the mother of vices. It developed in the men sloth, improvidence, servility; in the women, fawning and impurity. In the masters it developed arrogance, pride, and cruelty. As a system, it stands condemned at the bar of the world's best public opinion as utterly irreconcilable with correct principles of political economy, morality, or religion.

The Africans who were brought to this country as slaves were black, full-blooded Negroes; were ignorant, superstitious, and very degraded—Africa, whence they came, being mostly a land of barbarism. **A Blessing Deeply Disguised** Strange as it may seem, it is true that slavery, notwithstanding its evils, was in large degree overruled to their good. They learned to speak the English language. They learned that great and blessed lesson how to work. They became acquainted with the white man's ways, acquired a taste for freedom and real prosperity, and an intense desire for learning. When the Civil War began, in 1861, there were about four million slaves, but of these only a very small number were originally Africans (the slave trade having been stopped), and among them were a large number of mulattoes, or mixed bloods, some of whom were almost entirely white. These four million slaves, multitudes of whom through the preaching of the gospel and religious instruction had become Christians, were far removed in most respects from the degraded condition of the first shiploads of captives that were brought from Africa.

Emancipation

From the very first introduction of slavery there were those who looked upon the institution as wrong, but it was suffered to remain and grow until the evils of it became very many and very manifest. Some of the wisest and best people in the South considered it not only a moral wrong, but an economic evil, and believed that the country would be more prosperous without it than with it. When, however, the sentiment against it in the North became very strong, and efforts were made to prevent by legislation its spread

Slavery and Freedom

into new Territories and States, the question became a political one, and the South united almost solidly in advocating both its continuance and its extension. Some said that it could not be abolished; that the Negroes were unfit for freedom; that, if set free, they would miserably perish, and that the abolition of slavery would produce such a revolution in the condition of the South as would threaten that entire region with the greatest evils, economic, social, and political. Some very curious arguments were used in its favor: one was that God intended the Negroes to be slaves, and hence made them black; another, that all working people should be slaves, so that they could be better controlled by their masters; still another, that the white race would reach a higher stage of civilization by holding the blacks in slavery. Some went so far as to declare that Negroes were not human beings, but beasts; that they had no souls; but these people would have found it very difficult to explain such a phenomenon as Fred Douglas.

In the North there slowly grew up a very strong public sentiment in favor of the entire abolition of slavery, and those who advocated this action were called "Abolitionists." They formed themselves into clubs and societies, published newspapers, pamphlets, books, made addresses, wrote letters, and in a great variety of ways strove very earnestly to create a sentiment against slavery strong enough to overthrow it. William Lloyd Garrison, Wendell Phillips, Owen Lovejoy, Charles Sumner, and Henry Ward Beecher, were among the leading champions of the freedom of the slaves. Harriet Beecher Stowe published "Uncle Tom's Cabin," depicting the horrors of slavery, which had an enormous circulation and exerted a profound influence, notwithstanding the fact that many Southern people insisted that the picture was overdrawn, and that slavery was not so bad as she described it.

The Abolitionists

In 1856 the Free Soilers, as they were called, had acquired force enough in politics to secure the nomination of General John C. Fremont as the Republican candidate for the presidency, and, although he was not elected, he received a great many votes. The campaign in his behalf intensified the public sentiment against slavery, and, in consequence of this, in 1860,

Slavery and Freedom

Abraham Lincoln, of Illinois, was elected president of the United States. Many of the prominent politicians of the South professed to see in his election an act of hostility to slavery and an encroachment upon the rights of the Southern people, and they finally induced a large number of the States to try to secede from the Union and form a confederate government. The fundamental principle of the secession movement was the doctrine of State rights: that every State of the Union had the right to secede whenever the people thought it best for their own interest.

One of the principal motives that led to the formation of a confederacy was the protection and perpetuation of slavery. The secession movement led to one of the most disastrous wars ever waged, which continued from April, 1861, to April, 1865, and cost both the North and the South the expenditure of an enormous quantity of blood and treasure. The war was begun by the South. President Lincoln immediately called into service, first, seventy-five thousand volunteer soldiers; and he continued to call for new troops as long as they were needed, until the war was ended. His purpose, and that of the great army that he called into existence, was not to destroy slavery, but to preserve the Union. From the first, however, the Abolitionists, and many others, believed that the war begun for the perpetuation of slavery could end in no other way than in its destruction, and some were in favor of taking immediate steps for this.

President Abraham Lincoln, after a great deal of discussion and very much urging from the Abolitionists and others, **The Great Proclamation** finally, after having given warning of what he intended to do, unless those in rebellion against the government laid down their arms, issued on January 1, 1863, his famous Emancipation Proclamation, which declared free all slaves held in the States, or parts of States, still in rebellion against the national government. He issued this act as a war measure. As president of the United States, he was commander-in-chief of the army and the navy, and had a right to emancipate the slaves if thereby he could weaken the power of those who were trying to destroy the Union, and thus contribute to the preservation of the life of the Republic. By this act, and by subsequent legislation, all the slaves became free, and can never again be enslaved. By a change in the Constitution they were enfranchised, *i. e.*, they were allowed the privilege of voting and holding office the same as white men. These two acts, emancipation and enfranchisement, together mark a great epoch, or new starting-point, in the history of the Africans in America; heretofore, they had been slaves that could be bought and sold just as cattle are bought and sold, without any rights which the white man was bound to respect; hereafter they were to be free men and women, entitled to all the rights and privileges of American citizenship. This was a very great change, in their situation. Many people thought that they would die if thus set free; that they would become absolutely poor; that they could not care for themselves; that they would become lawless desperadoes. But, happily, no one of these things has proved to be true.

The Negroes did not fully understand what the Civil War meant. They could not read and their masters purposely kept them in ignorance as to the real state of things. There **Negroes in the War** was, however, a very general impression among them that the "Yankees" were their friends, and many of them believed that the Union army was coming South to set them free, but, of course, they could not express openly their desire for freedom, nor their hopes for the coming of "Massa Linkum's soldiers." Some of them had very absurd notions about Northern people; they had been told, and some of them actually believed, that the Yankee soldiers had horns, and it was very amusing to see the curious expression on their faces when they had their first sight of Union soldiers. Notwithstanding all the excitement occasioned by the war, the great body of the slaves remained quietly at home following their ordinary pursuits. A very large proportion of the able-bodied white men were in the Southern army, so that in numerous cases the white women and children were left alone with the Negro servants. The food for the families and the supplies for the Southern army were raised chiefly by the labor of the slaves, and it is an interesting fact that there were very few cases of complaint on the part of white women and children against them during the war. They seemed to feel that they were entrusted with the care of the white folks and took a pride in being faithful to their trust.

Slavery and Freedom

There were instances in which white women, on the approach of the Northern armies, confided to the keeping of their slaves their money, jewels, and other valuable property which they feared might fall into the hands of the soldiers; they rarely betrayed even this trust.

In many cases Southern white officers took their body servants with them into the army, where they remained for the most part loyal and faithful. Their good conduct at home during the war served to awaken a great deal of gratitude and admiration for them on the part of the white people of the South. If the Negroes had been so disposed, they had it in their power to work great harm during the absence of their masters and to inflict irreparable injury on the helpless women and children.

A very considerable number left their homes and passed the lines of the Union army. Some of them did this thinking they might immediately gain their freedom, **"Contrabands"** having very extravagant and crude notions of what freedom meant. Quite a number found employment in the Union army as cooks and waiters, but most of them had a hard time of it. General Benjamin F. Butler justified himself in seizing upon the slaves "because," he said, "they were contraband of war"; and so they came to be almost universally called "Contrabands." The places where they were herded together to be fed and cared for were called "Contraband camps." Their poverty, ignorance, and helplessness at once excited the pity of philanthropic people in the North and teachers and missionaries were sent among them; but not much could be done, because these camps were temporary and soon broken up.

After a great deal of discussion, in which much was said both for and against it, President Lincoln decided to enlist Negro troops for the Union army. This was one way of finding employment for the able-bodied men, who were very much better off with something to do than if they remained idle. Besides this, the wages that they would earn as soldiers would enable them to do something toward caring for their families and other friends who were dependent upon them for support. At first it was feared that they would not make good soldiers because they were so ignorant and so servile in disposition. It was thought,

Slavery and Freedom

however, that if they were properly organized and drilled they would at least be useful in constructing fortifications and in guarding military posts, thus relieving an equal number of veteran white soldiers who could take their places at the front to do the fighting. There were those who believed from the first that they would make good soldiers; that they were imitative, teachable, ambitious to excel, proud of being called men and treated as soldiers, and very desirous of doing something toward gaining their own liberties. The result showed that they were right. Nearly two hundred thousand Negro troops were organized, some as infantry, some as cavalry, and some as light and heavy artillery; they performed all kinds of military duty, took part in many hard-fought battles, and showed themselves to be in many respects admirable soldiers. They became very skillful in the manual of arms; learned all the movements of the soldier in companies, regiments, and brigades; kept their clothes, their arms, and their camps in good condition; stood very well the fatigue and hardships of heavy marches; were patient under wounds and sickness; endured quietly the hunger and other deprivations incident to army life; were obedient to their officers; were very brave in battle; and were thoughtful and kind toward white Southern prisoners whom they captured. Although they were not so intelligent and hence not so independent and self-reliant as most of the white soldiers of the Union army, they made a good record for themselves, and Negro troops have formed a part of the regular army ever since the close of the war.

At first there was a great deal of prejudice against them on the part of the white soldiers, but gradually this prejudice wore away and Negro troops were treated with the same respect and confidence as white troops. In some instances white regiments said that they would rather march and fight by the side of well-drilled, brave Negro regiments than with any other.

Naturally there was much indignation in the South because the North had organized slaves into regiments of soldiers, and many threats were made that if Negro troops were captured in battle they would be killed without mercy, and their officers would share the same fate. These threats, however, only made the colored soldiers more careful and more courageous, and stimulated their white officers to greater diligence in drilling them for service, and in preventing their being captured. The prejudice of even Southern soldiers and people against them gradually wore away, and there were very few instances in which those taken prisoners were treated with exceptional cruelty.

When the Negroes had been emancipated and enfranchised, the appalling fact presented itself of four million American citizens, without education and without political experience. *The Negroes in School* Here they were, just emerging from bondage, blinded by the glittering light of freedom, without experience, without leadership. Here were numbers of churches with pastors who could not read a word of the Bible they were trying to explain ; here were multitudes of children who ought to be in Sunday-school, but who had no teachers ; here was a great host of young people growing up without knowledge, deprived of the care of their masters because they were free, and having nobody to provide for them ; they were, indeed, like sheep without a shepherd, and unless something were done for them they would speedily fall a prey to ravening wolves.

The government organized what was called the "Freedmen's Bureau," and placed at the head of it General O. O. Howard, a Christian gentleman, a philanthropist, a brave soldier, and a broad-minded statesman. For several years this bureau labored earnestly and efficiently to improve the welfare of the Negroes, and accomplished great good. The government did not undertake to establish schools directly, but the bureau encouraged all educational movements among them.

Even before the war closed the philanthropic people of the North sent missionaries and teachers to labor among the "Contrabands," and in many of the important cities of most of the Southern States there were established Christian schools, having at first special reference to giving a rudimentary education to those who intended to preach. It was felt that the preachers ought at least to be able to read the Bible, as well as to know something of what the Bible taught. The work of these schools was necessarily, in the beginning, very primitive. They were attended at first by a good many old men, who, with their spectacles on, pored over their spelling lessons like little children in the primary department.

Slavery and Freedom

But even with these crude beginnings they accomplished from the outset a very important work; the teachers met the pupils not only in their class-rooms, where they learned to read and write and spell, but they taught them a great many useful things besides, and so helped them to do the work they were called upon to perform. These schools were at first held in some instances in Negro cabins, in other cases in the dark, damp basements of Negro churches.

Thirty-five years have gone by since these institutions were started, and the change that has taken place in them is wonderful indeed. To-day the Baptists alone are assist- **A Great Revolution** ing in supporting more than thirty of them for the Negroes in the South. One of these is a high-grade theological seminary, at Richmond, Va., where more than fifty young men are pursuing a course of study similar to that pursued in the best theological seminaries in the North. Another is Shaw University, at Raleigh, N. C., where there is an academic department, a normal department, a college, a school of pharmacy, a law school, and a medical school. This one institution has accomplished for the State of North Carolina a work that is very difficult to describe on account of its extent and importance. One of the greatest schools of the kind in the world is Spelman Seminary, at Atlanta, Ga., where there is a beautiful campus, a number of splendid brick buildings, a large faculty, and a great body of Negro girls and women. They are instructed in cooking, sewing, housekeeping; are taught typesetting; are trained as nurses for the sick room; are fitted to become missionaries, and there is a well-equipped normal school where they are educated for high-grade work as teachers. There are other schools, at Nashville, Tenn., Columbia, S. C., Marshall, Texas, and elsewhere. During the last year more than five thousand pupils were in attendance, and it is the testimony of all who are acquainted with them that the students are industrious and capable. Those who have gone out from these institutions to become teachers, pastors, lawyers, doctors, editors, and to fill other useful occupations, are among the foremost men and women of the race, and are doing an invaluable work for their people.

The Baptists of the North have expended in this educational work, since the war, more than three million dollars, and they are spending now more than a hundred thousand dollars every year to carry it on.

The Negroes have organized schools at Louisville, Ky.; Selma, Ala.; Little Rock, Ark.; Macon, Mo.; Augusta, Ga.; Lynchburg, Va., and elsewhere, which they are conducting themselves. **Negro Schools** They are under the control of Negro Boards of Trustees, are taught by Negro faculties, and most of the money needed for their support is contributed by the Negroes. Nearly all of them, however, receive some help from the American Baptist Home Mission Society.

Of the eight million Negroes now in the country more than one million six hundred thousand are members of Baptist churches, and a great many more are in sympathy with the Baptists, and naturally look to them for aid in missionary and educational work. The Negroes are poor, and are not yet able to carry on their educational work without help, and one of the most beneficent schemes ever devised and carried on by Christian people anywhere in the world at any time, is that of establishing among them these Christian schools of learning for the development of their manhood and womanhood, the formation of their Christian character, and the preparation for usefulness of thousands and tens of thousands of those who are to be leaders of their race.

Many others besides the Baptists have been and are engaged in this important work, among them being the Congregationalists, Methodists, and Presbyterians. Some of the great schools they have established and fostered are Hampton Institute in Virginia, Fisk University in Nashville, Straight University at New Orleans, Biddle University in North Carolina, Clarke and Atlanta Universities in Georgia, and Tuskeegee Institute in Alabama.

In addition to the work done by the religious denominations, the most important help furnished to Negro education by persons not living in the South has been given through the Peabody and Slater Funds, which comprise several million dollars. The first secretary of this great beneficent educational fund was a Northern man, Rev. Dr. Barnas Sears, once president of Brown University; the next two were the late Dr. Haygood, of Georgia, and Hon. J. L. M. Curry, of Virginia, both Southern men and both very earnest, intelligent, and faithful in disbursing the money for the best interests of all concerned. The Slater Fund was exclusively for the benefit of the Negroes, while the Peabody Fund was for all.

Besides the philanthropic work inaugurated by Northern capital, there has now been established in all the Southern States a public school system for the equal benefit of white and Negro children. **The Public Schools** In the North, colored children can attend all schools and colleges and universities, but in the South they have separate schools and are not allowed to attend any others. The young Negroes of the South, therefore, do not have the same opportunity for acquiring a liberal education that white children have either in the South or North. Their public schools are, as yet, not of a high order, being taught almost entirely by Negroes, very many of whom are but poorly prepared for their work. The schoolhouses, especially in the country, are poor; they are not well supplied with books or apparatus, and the schools continue only a few months in the year. Nevertheless, they are accomplishing a great deal of good, and are being improved from year to year, so that by and by they will probably become very efficient. The great body of Negro children must depend upon the public schools for their education, hence these schools should have the sympathy and support of all classes of people. The Southern States are entitled to great credit for what has already been done in this work.

One of the most hopeful factors in the development of the Negro race, the improvement of their material and moral condition, has been their thirst for knowledge. This was particularly characteristic of those who had been slaves, whom it was unlawful to teach to read and write, and who were thus shut out from even the simplest rudiments of a common English education. They were almost universally eager to get an education, and when the opportunity was presented not only multitudes of adults, but many old men and women, took their places along with little children in schoolrooms. While there are marked exceptions not a few, yet it is still true of the Negroes as a body that they are anxious to learn.

In Africa there is an immense number of

Slavery and Freedom

Negroes, how many nobody knows, but probably not less than one hundred and fifty or two hundred millions. Some of these apparently have no religion at all; many are idolaters, some Mohammedans, and a very few are Christians. **Negro Christians** Of the eight millions in this country, a very large proportion belong to Christian churches; one million six hundred thousand are reported to be members of Baptist churches, about the same number are enrolled in Methodist churches, and besides these there are Presbyterians, Congregationalists, Episcopalians, and others. It is a singular fact that perhaps a larger proportion of Negroes are enrolled as church-members than of any other class of people, and in this respect the contrast between the Africans in America and those in Africa is very striking.

In the days of slavery they usually attended the same churches as their masters, being allowed to sit in the back seats or in the galleries, where they listened to the preaching of the gospel. Many of them were converted and were received as members of white churches. Services were frequently held especially for them, and many eminent Southern preachers took great satisfaction in preaching to them.

After the war the Negro Christians almost universally separated themselves from their white brethren and formed churches of their own; they preferred to have Negro pastors, to carry on their own religious work, and to conduct their services in their own fashion. There has been very naturally a good deal of very crude preaching and some strange customs in connection with their religious worship. They are an emotional people, fond of excitement, and oftentimes in their churches they give themselves up to a kind of religious frenzy, shouting, screaming and doing many things which seem very strange to outsiders. It ought to be said, however, that in some cases they have copied these curious customs from white people, and that even to-day there are white congregations whose manner of worship is quite as grotesque as theirs. It should also be especially remembered that there is a great improvement in this respect, and to-day very many of their congregations are as quiet, orderly, and decorous as those made up of highly cultivated white people.

At first their pastors were ignorant and their

preaching of a very poor quality. At the present time, however, there are found many Negro pastors who have been well educated, some in schools, some in colleges, and some in theological seminaries, whose preaching is intelligent, biblical, earnest, and effective. Indeed, some of them are eloquent and preach sermons remarkable for their oratorical power. They have vivid imaginations, a surprising command of language (which is not always used with exactness), and they frequently preach with extraordinary fervor. They usually assume a larger degree of authority over their churches and rule their congregations much more absolutely than pastors of intelligent white churches are wont to do; but this evil will correct itself as the members of the churches grow in intelligence, independence, and the power of self-government.

When the war closed the Negroes had very few and very poor houses of worship, but now all through the South are to be found meeting-houses which they have built, chiefly with their own money, and many of them are large, comfortable, convenient, and even costly. It is remarkable and much to their credit that they have been willing, out of their small earnings, to contribute such large amounts to build meeting-houses.

It is sometimes asserted that their religion does not always control their action; that their profession is better than their practice, which is probably true of Christians generally. We should remember that under the system of slavery they imbibed very erroneous notions of morality. They did not think it wrong to steal from their masters, because they were only helping themselves to what they had produced by their toil; they could not see why it was right for the white men to take possession of them, buy and sell them like cattle, and appropriate to their own use, without their consent, all that they earned by their labor. Among free, intelligent people the family and the home are sacred. The relations of husband and wife, parent and child, brother and sister, are very sweet and tender, and are the foundation of noble characters. Among the slaves there could be no families, and all these dear relations were disregarded and trampled upon, so that the standard of morality and the rules of conduct common in Christian families would be unknown among

Religion and Right Living

Slavery and Freedom

slaves. When they became free, so that the husband could have his own wife and the parents could care for their own children, a new order of things was introduced. But necessarily it takes a great deal of time to develop ideas of morality which are permanent and forceful in regulating conduct, although they are making rapid and hopeful progress in this direction.

There is needed among them a very much larger number of pious, able men who have been well educated and especially trained for the office of pastor. One fact will serve to show how great is this need: There are in the North about one million white Baptists, and there are five great theological seminaries where young men are trained to be pastors, and this is not too many. There are in the South one million six hundred thousand Negro Baptists, and there is only one solitary Baptist theological seminary to furnish for their churches a well-educated ministry. There ought to be at least two more, one at Atlanta, Ga., and one at Marshall, Texas, and there would be, if money could be found to establish and maintain them.

Need of an Educated Ministry

The development of the moral and religious life of any people is very difficult and necessarily very slow; many generations must pass away before it can be accomplished. It is now nearly one thousand nine hundred years since the establishment of Christianity upon the earth, and even the most favored white people who have enjoyed the best opportunities have not yet embodied in their lives, individually and collectively, the teachings and spirit of Jesus Christ. It was not to be expected that the Negroes would make much greater progress in their moral and religious growth than has been made by white people under even more favorable circumstances. Those who are best acquainted with them believe that they will develop a high type of religious life. They are fond of music; many of them greatly excel as singers, and no doubt they will attain to a high order of sacred music in their churches. They are a sympathetic and liberal people, which will lead them to be generous in their contributions for the care of the sick and poor and for sending the gospel to the heathen. Their pulpit oratory, while conforming more and more to accepted standards among white people, will doubtless retain for generations something of its own fervor and rhetorical embellishments. They have as yet very much to learn regarding effective organization for educational, religious, and missionary work, but in this too they are making fair progress, and education, experience, and time will do for them what it has done for others.

We are now entering upon what promises to be an era of co-operation in behalf of the evangelization and education of the Negroes. There are several very distinct stages which mark the progress of this people in America, to some of which allusion has already been made. First, there was the barbaric heathenism in which they lived in their native land; then there were two hundred and fifty years of American bondage in which they acquired a forced acquaintance with the rudiments of civilization; this was followed by the stage of helplessness incident upon their sudden liberation from bondage while unprepared for freedom. During this stage they could do very little for their own moral or intellectual improvement and were dependent chiefly upon the missionaries and teachers who were sent to them from the North. Most of

Co-operation

the white people of the South felt aggrieved because the Negroes had been set free; they were impoverished by the dreadful war, and many of them were much embittered against both the Negroes and the North because their former slaves had not only been emancipated, but also enfranchised. They could not be expected at once to enter heartily into the work of providing schools for their proper education, and for many years those established by the Northerners found little favor among them. The teachers who went South were not generally received into good society, and were classed with the people they came to teach. Unfortunately this social ostracism is not yet wholly a thing of the past.

In some cases the Negroes have been a little restive under the work done for them by their Northern friends, and have urged very strongly that more of their own number should be employed as teachers and members of Boards of trustees, in extreme cases even insisting that the schools established for them by Northern philanthropy and money should be turned over to their exclusive management. But it requires a great deal of wisdom and experience to manage educational institutions successfully, and those who have done most for the establishment of these schools in the South have felt that the interest of the Negroes themselves would be best promoted by having their management continue in the hands of their founders. It has not been easy to reconcile these conflicting policies, but time is a great healer and is doing its beneficent work in this as in other cases.

Some extremists among the Negroes are in favor of drawing the color line; that is, they wish to separate themselves as far as possible from white people; they strongly insist that they ought to prosecute their own missionary work, publish their own literature, manage their own schools, and not be dependent in any respect upon white people, against whom they have a strong race prejudice. This is a very foolish attitude. "God made of one blood all nations of the earth," and one of the ripest fruits of Christianity, and one of the most precious results of Christian civilization, is the destruction of the race barriers between different peoples. The destiny of the Negroes in America is indissolubly linked with that of the white people. The present

Drawing the Color Line

generation of them owe the progress which they have made since emancipation largely to the help afforded them by white people ; unaided they never could have established for themselves the schools which have done so much for them. They have not been able to properly equip, much less to endow, a single school for themselves. If the white Baptists, who have expended already more than three million dollars for their benefit, and are to-day making an annual expenditure of more than one hundred thousand dollars for the support of their schools and the promotion of missionary work, should withdraw their support, it would be an unspeakable calamity. After the Negroes have done all that they possibly can do to help themselves, and after the white people have done all that they can be induced to do, the Negroes will still be without the educational advantages and religious privileges which they very greatly need. To Christianize and educate eight million people is a herculean task and calls for the united effort of all uplifting forces. Instead of seeking to separate between the white and the black people of this country, every effort should be made to unite them closer and closer in all that looks toward the education and Christianization of the Negroes.

The educational and missionary work which the Northern Baptists are doing for the Negroes is carried on especially by four great organizations—the American Baptist Home Mission Society, the American Baptist Publication Society, the Women's Home Mission Society of New England, and the Women's Home Mission Society of Chicago. The New England Women's Society is now co-operating very fully with the parent Society in New York; the Western Women's Society co-operates in part.

A movement is now in progress looking toward the organization of Negro State education societies to co-operate heartily with the Home Mission Society in organizing, unifying, and rendering efficient all Negro educational work. This plan is in very successful operation in Virginia, Tennessee, Georgia, and Mississippi; it is expected that other Southern States will very quickly follow their lead.

There is also a plan of co-operation which unites the Home Mission Society, the Home Board of the Southern Baptist Convention, the white State Convention, and the Negro State

Conventions, in carrying on, especially, missionary work among the Negroes. A very important series of "New Era Institutes" are being held, where lectures are delivered by both white and colored pastors, and where a great deal of good is being done in fitting pastors, Sunday-school superintendents, teachers, and others for more effective Christian work. This plan is now in successful operation in Virginia, North and South Carolina, Alabama, Kentucky, and Missouri, and it is hoped and believed that before a great while all the Baptist forces of the North and South will be working together to promote the highest moral, religious, and intellectual interests of the Negroes.

The progress of any people from a state of savagery up through barbarism to a high stage of civilization is a complex and tedious one. The ancestors of the white people now living in America were savages many centuries ago, and our present civilization is the result of many co-operating forces. No race or people has ever attained high civilization without outside help, and the highest civilization is impossible without co-operation. If the Negroes in America are ever to become highly civilized, so as to participate in all the advantages and privileges of modern science, philosophy, politics, and religion, they must have the sympathy and the help of white people. At the same time they must do all they can to help themselves, and not only this, if they are to reach the highest stage of life, they must help other people. No nation or people can become great in the true sense who concentrate their efforts upon themselves. It is just as true of people and nations as it is of individuals, that "no man liveth to himself."

Very many more things of interest might be said concerning the Negroes in America, their political life, their industries, what they have done in music, poetry, painting, etc., and something too about their social ostracism and the cruelties to which they are subjected at the hands of mobs, etc., but limits of space forbid. A word, however, must be said about their young people. There is now a host of several thousand Baptist young people belonging to the white Baptist churches of the North, and multitudes of these have allied themselves with the Young People's Union. Connected with the Negro Baptist churches in the South

Negro Baptist Young People

are nearly twice as many young people as are found among the white churches in the North, and some of these have also formed themselves into unions. The work of organization has not been carried forward among them as it has among the white young people of the North, and very few attend the great National Conventions; this is true partly because not many of them can afford to spend their little means in taking long journeys.

A great deal of good is being accomplished among the Baptist Young People through the Union. Those who are pursuing the Christian Culture Courses carefully are acquiring much valuable information about Christianity, about Baptist churches and Baptist history, which will be very useful to them as individual Christians and as workers in the churches. The Negro Baptist Young People need the same kind of education as their white brothers and sisters are acquiring. They have the same talents, the same sort of religious duties to perform, and they will be benefited by the Christian Culture Courses and by association together in local churches, in State conventions, and in the great national assemblies, precisely in the same manner as if they were white. Twenty-

Slavery and Freedom

five years from now, as things are going at present, it looks as though there would be as many Negro Baptists in America as there are white Baptists, in both the North and the South. Indeed, it will not be surprising if before the end of the present century, which is now very near, there will be more than two million Negro Baptists. It is very important, therefore, simply on the ground of numbers, that the young men and young women growing up in these Baptist churches should be well educated and well trained for Christian service, in order that they may be useful members of society, and be able to meet the great responsibilities that the twentieth century will impose upon them.

If the millions and millions of Negroes now living in heathenism on the continent of Africa are ever to be reached by the gospel, it looks as though it would have to be done by the young men and women now growing up in the Negro churches of this country. What a wonderful thing it would be if during the next hundred years there could go back to heathen Africa shiploads of missionaries to preach the gospel on

A Plea from Africa

the Dark Continent, instead of the shiploads of poor slaves that were brought from Africa to America during the last century. Perhaps some of the readers of this book will live to see that great event. Already there is coming to us from Africa an earnest plea for missionaries. Ethiopia is stretching out her hand. God in his providence seems to be preparing the hearts of the Africans for the reception of the gospel, and is also apparently preparing in this country hosts of young men and women who will be glad to go and give it to those who are sitting in darkness.

Our fathers snatched the unwilling Negro captives away from their native land, their kindred, their friends, brought them here and sold them into slavery; they and their children toiled, not for their own benefit, but for the benefit of their masters; they created the wealth which others enjoyed. God in his providence raised up Abraham Lincoln to be their deliverer, and through him struck from their limbs the shackles of bondage. They are now free men and free women, citizens of the American Republic; nearly two millions of them are Baptists, our brethren in the Lord; we have a common Father in heaven,

Slavery and Freedom

and they have a right to expect of us kindness and help. When they are educated and have become prosperous they will repay us for all that we do for them, not perhaps by aiding us, but by sending the gospel to Africa, and helping to win for Christ in that dark continent a multitude of followers, "whom no man can number."

I do not mean to say that the regeneration of Africa is to be left entirely to the Negroes of America. The white Christians of this country are under obligation to do all in their power for the accomplishment of this mighty purpose, and they cannot shift the responsibility from their shoulders to those of their brethren in black. But it is nevertheless true that the Negroes are better adapted to endure the rigors of the climate and the deprivations incident to missionary life in Africa than white men are. Neither do I wish to be understood as saying or implying that the Negroes should content themselves with doing missionary work among Negroes. They are debtors to all the world as well as to Africa.

Each generation has its own great problems to solve. The century now nearing its end has been one of the most notable of all the series in the world's history; great things have been done; great progress has been made. It has been pre-eminently a century of scientific discoveries, of inventions, and of missions. Its crowning glory is the fact that so much has been done for the religious welfare of mankind. Doubtless the twentieth century will in many respects surpass the nineteenth. The young people now coming upon the stage of action may look forward to a most interesting career. Many new and strange questions will doubtless arise, calling both for profound thought and vigorous action. Happy they who shall enter this century well equipped to play their part in its great activities.

Twentieth Century Problems

Without any doubt one of the great questions that will insist upon solution during this next century will be that of the proper relation of the Negroes in America with their white fellow-citizens. Numbering now about eight millions, during the next century they will probably increase to seventy-five or a hundred millions. They are here to stay. They will remain an integral part of our national life. They will exert a tremendous influence, for

Slavery and Freedom

good or for evil. There is every reason why they should be educated and Christianized. If the white people do not lift the black people up, the black people will pull the white people down. It is manifestly to the interest of the white people themselves to do everything possible to foster education and Christianity among the Negroes, and to prepare the rising generation not only to become self-supporting, but to become efficient factors in promoting the common welfare of the nation.

II

NEGROES IN THE CIVIL WAR

At the outbreak of the war between the Northern and Southern States, in 1861, there were in the country, approximately, four million slaves. During the conflict nearly two hundred thousand Negroes were enrolled in the United States' army, comparatively few of whom were enlisted from among the free Negroes of the North. The great mass of them were slaves from the Southern plantations. The purpose of this chapter is to consider this fact in its relation to the present and probable status of the race in this country.

The great body of citizens in the North who sympathized with the purpose of President Lincoln to suppress the rebellion were actuated, primarily, by love for the Union and a determination to preserve its integrity at any cost. Patriotism was the battlecry of the hour. Among those who rallied to the support of the government in its hour of need were many

Negroes in the Civil War

Abolitionists who disliked slavery, who saw in the Civil War a possible means of its destruction, and rejoiced at the prospect. It is safe to say, however, that these were largely in the minority. The greater portion of the army was either indifferent to slavery or was in full sympathy with President Lincoln's purpose to save the Union with slavery if he could, without it if he must. In the early days of the war, many of the Union soldiers were quick to resent the taunt sometimes hurled at them that they were "fighting to free the Nigger."

When the armies moved South they came immediately into contact with the slaves, multitudes of whom flocked within the Union lines asking for service, protection, and support. For the most part they were a motley crew, many being in rags, and while some found employment, the most were herded together and supplied with the bare necessaries of life.

When the question was first broached of enlisting Negro soldiers there was a very strong prejudice against it among both officers and men. The general opinion seemed to be that slaves were disqualified for efficient service as soldiers by reason of their ignorance

The Great Debate

and the servile spirit begotten by bondage. They could not be expected to be brave, it was said, especially when brought face to face with their former masters whom they had been taught to respect, reverence, and obey. The introduction of any considerable number of such recruits was almost universally regarded as an experiment full of hazard, and to be tried only as a last resort. Among the private soldiers the feeling prevailed that it would be disgraceful to have Negro slaves enlisted and put into the army on the same footing as themselves, and murmurs of discontent at the proposition and threats of desertion if it were carried out were frequently heard. Besides this, there was also a strong objection to arming the slaves and using them as soldiers to fight their old masters on the ground that it savored a little of dishonor; and, further, that it would necessarily intensify the bitterness of the Southern soldiers and people against the Union army and the North.

On the other hand, those among the officers and soldiers who favored their enlistment argued that one of the probable results of the war was to be the destruction of slavery, that consequently the slaves had more at stake than any

Negroes in the Civil War

other class of persons, and hence, that they should share the burden of the war and aid in the suppression of the rebellion. Then too, if they were to be free, their experience as soldiers would prepare them for freedom as no other experience possibly could. Few people in the history of the world have ever gained their freedom except by fighting. It was also urged that they were essentially imitative and obedient, that they were fond of dress and of show, and would be particularly susceptible as soldiers to the "pomp, parade, and glorious circumstance of war." The certainty of their severe treatment if captured in battle would be an added stimulus to desperate courage. The fact that thousands of them were serving as officers' servants had indirectly proved a wonderful preparation for service as soldiers, for, although non-combatants, they had learned much by observation of the duties, trials, and dangers of army life. As the war progressed and the destruction of human life became more and more serious, there were not a few who sympathized with Miles O'Reily's sentiment that "The right to be kill't he'd divide with the Naygur, and give him the bigger half." As it was often tersely put by the soldiers, "a black man would stop a rebel bullet just as well as a white man," and at length the opinion of the army came to be that Negro soldiers, organized and disciplined, could at least perform, as has been said, invaluable service in the construction of fortifications and the guarding of forts, thus liberating for service in the field an equal number of veteran white troops.

In due time the enlistment of colored troops was fully decided upon by the government; camps were established and the work of organization began. The policy was adopted of selecting from the Negroes themselves all non-commissioned officers, while commissioning as field and line officers only white men, to be selected chiefly from officers and soldiers who had already seen service. The general principle was followed of selecting officers for colored troops by competitive examination, and this resulted in securing for the most part men who were well qualified for their work. Unhappily, as might be expected, some who were actuated chiefly by personal ambition found their way into official positions in this service—as a certain colonel of my acquaintance expressed it, he "cared nothing for the 'niggers,' except for the army rank they en-

Negroes in the Civil War

abled him to attain." It is needless to say that his success as a commanding officer of Negro troops was not brilliant.

I entered the colored service in October, 1863, having been promoted, after examination, from first lieutenant, in the Seventieth Indiana Regiment commanded by Colonel Benjamin Harrison, to the rank of major in the Fourteenth United States Colored Infantry. I organized the regiment and became its colonel; organized also the Forty-second and Forty-fourth Regiments of United States Colored Infantry; commanded at different times more than five thousand Negro troops; was with them in battle at Dalton, Ga.; Decatur, Ala.; Franklin and Nashville, Tenn. At the last named place it was my privilege to open the great battle with a brigade of Negro troops and a brigade of white troops, constituting a provisional division. My superior officer was Gen. James B. Steadman, who was in command of the left wing of the Army of the Cumberland, commanded by Gen. George H. Thomas. I thus had the opportunity of seeing a good deal of service, and making a pretty careful study of Negro soldiers under very favorable circumstances.

Among so large a number of troops, so widely scattered over such a broad theatre of military operations, under circumstances which varied so greatly, there would necessarily be wide differences among Negro troops, as there would be among white troops, and any general statements are true—subject to qualifications. Very much depended, necessarily, upon the courage and general character of the white officers who were appointed to drill, discipline, and lead them. As the war closed in April, 1865, there was not time enough to settle definitely and permanently the question of their soldierly qualities. The general ignorance which prevailed among them, very few being able to either read or write, militated very much against their highest efficiency. The contrast between the average intelligence of many of the white regiments of the Union army—recruited from the best men of the North—farmers' sons, clerks, schoolteachers, and thrifty business men—and a regiment made up of Negroes just out of bondage, was very striking. The high character of the men composing the Union army is well known. No less than six of its officers have been presi-

Characteristics of Negro Troops

Negroes in the Civil War

dents of the United States, scores of them have been senators and governors, and large numbers have filled other high official stations. The private soldiers have been found in all the honorable walks of life—civil and political, commercial, educational, and religious. No such body of intelligent men was ever before enrolled in an army, and its effectiveness was due largely to the high average of its intelligence, as was the superiority of the German army over the French army in their late war. While the cardinal virtue of the soldier is obedience, every experienced army officer well knows that the greater the intelligence among private soldiers, the greater their efficiency in actual war. Among the liberated slaves who were enlisted as soldiers there were numbers of stalwart men, some of them mixed bloods who had enjoyed exceptional advantages, and who possessed a fair degree of general intelligence. Many of these men, after preliminary instruction and training, rendered efficient service as sergeants, and acquired considerable skill as drill-masters.

In very many of the colored regiments schools of instruction were established for giving the soldiers the elements of an English education;

large numbers of them availed themselves most eagerly of the privilege of learning to read and write. They showed themselves apt in acquiring a knowledge of tactics, and some of them came to use their arms with exceptional skill. Gen. George H. Thomas, a graduate of West Point, and an experienced soldier, said of the Fourteenth United States Colored Infantry, that it handled its arms better than any other regiment he had ever seen. The courage of Negro soldiers was vindicated and thoroughly established on many a battlefield. I had a somewhat wide and varied experience in the army, was in several heavy engagements, commanded both white and black troops, and now, as I look back upon it, after a third of a century, I am somewhat in doubt as to which class of troops, white or black, I should give preference for courage. The blacks were perhaps more dependent upon their officers than white troops were; possibly possessed less of sustained courage under trying circumstances, but they endured pain with wonderful fortitude, and were capable of romantic heroism, such as they exhibited at Petersburg. The fact that several regiments of Negro troops were incorporated into the regular army, where they have been continued ever since the war, is pretty conclusive evidence that they possess soldierly qualities.

The near and remote consequences resulting from their enlistment in the Union army were many and important. One of the most obvious is that it gave employment to nearly two hundred thousand able-bodied men who had been thrown out of their former service by the progress of the war and had, as yet, found no place of independent labor. In addition to giving them something to do, it afforded food, clothing, protection, and wages, which many of them used either in the support of their families or in the assistance of relatives or friends who were partially dependent upon them, and it was vastly better that they should earn this help from the government than that they should receive it as a gratuity. It further served to greatly stimulate a healthful self-respect. They are not wanting in natural pride and ambition, which even in slavery was a spur to success and a solace in sorrow. The tendency of slavery, however, was to degrade them, or, at least to keep them degraded; to stifle the natural craving after recognition of

Results of Negro Enlistment

their manhood and the rewards that follow such recognition. Slavery begets cringing, fawning cowardice. They entertained exaggerated notions of the dignity of soldiers, and looked upon the Union army as a heroic band of conquering heroes with whom it would be an honor to serve, even in the humblest capacity. When they came to be enlisted as soldiers and to serve as a part of the great army of liberation, to wear a soldier's uniform, to carry a musket and be addressed as "men" and treated with respect, they felt that the "year of jubilee" had indeed come. When they had participated in hot engagements, such as those at Nashville, Petersburg, and Port Hudson, acquitting themselves valiantly and winning the praise of their officers and the encomium of white soldiers, they realized, not in its full significance, perhaps, but partially at least, that they had crossed the great gulf which separates between chattels and men. They had vindicated their manhood by the test which all the world has for centuries recognized as a severe one, the test of courage in battle.

It is to be recorded to the credit of the Negro soldiers that the instances were rare when they abused their powers. They "pick-

Negroes in the Civil War

eted" the lines through which Southern citizens passed and treated them courteously. They often guarded the property and families of Southern soldiers. They captured Confederates and held them as prisoners without injury or insult.

The increase in the Negroes' self-respect was surpassed by the increase of respect extended them by others. I have already spoken of the strong prejudice existing at **Removal of Prejudice** first against their enlistment as soldiers, and the sort of contempt with which they were looked upon, and it was my lot to witness a revolution in the public sentiment of the army in this particular. My regiment had a beautiful camp on the slope of the ridge near the Tennessee River, under the shadow of Lookout Mountain, in Chattanooga, Tenn. The camp was laid out with great regularity, was kept scrupulously clean; the men were well clothed and finely drilled; and when they appeared upon dress parade with their shoes blacked, their belts polished, their arms glistening, their clothes well brushed, with their white gloves, and went through their manual of arms with great precision, promptness, and enthusiasm, marching by companies from the parade ground under the command of Negro sergeants, they presented a most impressive spectacle. Tens of thousands of soldiers and citizens gathered to witness their parades, among them being a large portion of Sherman's army on its march to Atlanta. It was an object-lesson whose significance was striking, eloquent, and instantaneously effective, helping to rapidly change the sentiment of that whole Western army regarding Negro troops. The most common expression to be heard among the visitors after witnessing a parade was, "Those men will fight."

A signal instance of the prejudice which at first existed against Negro soldiers occurred at Nashville in the fall of 1863. At a public reception given by General Ward, an officer of a Negro regiment meeting an acquaintance, the lieutenant-colonel of an Ohio regiment, offered him his hand, which the latter declined, remarking as he turned away, that he "did not recognize Negro officers." When the matter reached the ears of Lorenzo Thomas, adjutant-general of the army, the offending officer was promptly dismissed from the service.

Our first engagement was at Dalton in Au-

Negroes in the Civil War

gust, 1864, when we had a sharp little contest with Wheeler's[1] cavalry. The Fifty-first Indiana Infantry fought on our flank, and was so impressed with the coolness and gallantry of my men that ever after that, by way of pleasantry and of compliment to the Negro soldiers, it was very common for its members when asked the usual question propounded by passing troops, "What regiment?" to reply, "Fifty-first Colored." After my soldiers had charged and taken a battery at Decatur, Ala., in October, 1864, and had shown great gallantry the following day under fire, they received an ovation from the white troops, who by thousands sprang upon the parapets and cheered the regiment as it re-entered the lines. The colonel of the Sixty-eighth Indiana Infantry asked from General Granger as a special privilege for his regiment, that it might be brigaded with mine, giving as a reason that his soldiers had such respect for the Fourteenth Colored that they wanted to fight side by side with it.

A First Fight

---

[1] What a comment on the changes of a quarter of a century, that this same General Wheeler commanded a division in the American army that captured Santiago.

Gen. George H. Thomas, a Virginian, and a man of great conservatism, was deeply interested in the work of organizing and disciplining Negro troops, frequently visiting my camp, inspecting the quarters, talking with me and conversing freely with the Negro soldiers. He once asked me if I thought they would fight, to which I of course replied: "Yes, general, they will." He said slowly: "Well, I think they would fight behind breastworks." And when I replied to this that I would prove that they would fight in the open field, if he would give me a chance, he answered quickly: "I will give you that chance." At the battle of Nashville, in the final charge on Overton's Hill, which pierced the enemy's line and precipitated his flight, black troops and white troops fought and fell side by side. As General Thomas and staff rode over the field after the battle and looked upon the fallen black soldiers he said to his officers: "The question is settled; Negro soldiers will fight." From that day on they had no firmer friend than he.

The addition of the Negro contingent to the Union army was immediately apparent in increasing its strength and effectiveness. In the early part of October, 1863, I began the organization of the fourteenth regiment at Gallatin, Tenn., and before the enlistments were completed or any company organizations effected, I was called upon by the commanding officer of the Post, Gen. E. A. Payne, to do picket duty. During the entire time occupied in the organization of the first six companies of the regiment we performed regular military duty, and as soon as the companies were fully organized, and before they had time for proper drill or discipline, we were ordered to Chattanooga, where the men were employed in the erection of fortifications and other service which had previously been performed by white soldiers. What was true of my regiment was true in large part of the entire force of Negro troops; every man of them counted one as an additional element of strength in the army. Not only did those actually enrolled add their strength to the force in the field, but the fact that they would make good soldiers, and that a very large number of them were available for that service, became at once an element of encouragement to the North in its stupendous work of putting down the rebellion. As the war proceeded it became more and more difficult to fill the ranks depleted by death, wounds, and disease, and there was a great public sense of relief and hope when this new source of supply was brought prominently forward.

While the addition of nearly two hundred thousand soldiers to the Union army was an immense factor of strength, encouragement, and hope for the North, it was no less a factor of discouragement to the South. The one great weakness of the Southern States in their effort to separate themselves from the Union was the lack of men. It was said of them that to recruit their armies they had robbed both the cradle and the grave—that is, that they had enlisted both very young and very old men. The far-sighted among them early appreciated the immense advantage which the North had in the mere force of numbers. When the experiment of organizing Negro troops had proven successful, the Southern people saw at once the full significance of this, since it took from their very homes the able-bodied, stalwart slaves, upon whom rested chiefly the burden of raising the crops which were to supply their armies, and converted them into an engine of destruc-

Two Hundred Thousand Soldiers

tion in the hands of their opponents. That the Negro contingent therefore exerted a profound influence in determining the ultimate issues of the war, and hastened the overthrow of the Confederacy, no one can doubt.

When it was over it was recognized by common consent that the Negroes had been an influential factor in preserving the integrity of the Union, and there was at once a spontaneous recognition of their right and claim to honorable and generous treatment. This was one of the great factors that led to their enfranchisement. In Congress and out it was argued that, as the States were to come back into the Union with their autonomy unimpaired, and that those who had been for nearly four years actively engaged in an effort to destroy it were to be re-invested with all the rights and privileges of American citizenship, it seemed only just and fitting that the Negroes, who had fought so courageously to preserve the Union, should share in these privileges. It was said also, with justice, that their latter condition might very naturally be worse than their first, if all the rights of citizenship were restored to their former masters while they were withheld from them. As they had fought against their masters on many a battlefield, and had thrown their immense weight in favor of the Union and for the overthrow of the Confederacy, it was only natural to suppose that the white people, restored to their political power, would be swift to visit upon their former slaves and late antagonists severe retribution. So it came about that Negro soldiers were the precursors of Negro citizens. It is not at all certain that they would have been enfranchised if they had not first been enlisted; indeed, if after enlistment, their services as soldiers had been discreditable, it is almost certain that the suffrage would have been withheld from them.

Whatever opinion may be cherished regarding the wisdom of conferring the right of suffrage upon the vast body of lately emancipated slaves, it must be conceded that enfranchisement marks an epoch in the evolution of the American Negro. He has retained the ballot until the present time, and there is no likelihood that it will ever be taken from him.

One of the immediate results of enfranchisement, and consequently one of the remoter results of enlistment as soldiers, was the education of the Negroes. The need of education for a free people had become an established truism in the American mind. If therefore the Negroes were to be free men, indeed, citizens of the Republic, vested with the power of the ballot, they too must be educated. This perhaps, quite as much as any other motive, if not the most powerful of all, has aided in establishing in the South, by Northern Christian philanthropy, large schools for the education of leaders among the colored people. It has also been influential in the creation through the South of the public school system, in whose advantages they participate.

Looking back upon this question of Negro soldiers after the lapse of a generation, I confess to a little feeling of disappointment in its effect upon them as a race. It is quite possible that I expected too much ; it may also be true that I do not as yet fully appreciate the ultimate influence of this single factor in their development. We have to remember that the four millions of slaves have grown to be more than eight millions of freemen ; that as a race they are not students of history, and hence have not been so profoundly influenced by the Negro army of liberation, as the American people in general have been influenced by the

Resumè

Revolutionary army, and that they are essentially a peaceable, docile, trusting, dependent race, not warlike, nor revengeful.

It is still further to be considered, in making an estimate of a historical fact such as that under consideration, that two hundred thousand black soldiers, although a large number in itself was really a very small number compared with the vast Union army of which it formed a part, and that they were officered by white men, who have received, possibly, more than their share of the credit attaching to the good conduct of the regiments which they commanded and led. The officers and soldiers of the Union army have been a dominating influence for a generation. The Loyal Legion and the Grand Army of the Republic have been factors of tremendous significance in the life of the nation. The national capital abounds in military statues, and expensive monuments have been erected there and in many other places to perpetuate the memory of those who gave their lives for their country. The Negro soldiers have had no great organization ; no monuments have been erected to perpetuate the memory of fallen heroes, and the influence that has been exerted upon the

Negroes in the Civil War

development of the race by those who fought during the Civil War has been incidental, indirect, and comparatively insignificant. This may be accounted for largely by the circumstances of the case : the Negro soldiers were illiterate, while thousands of the white men who enlisted in the Union army were graduates of colleges and universities, or were men who had already achieved distinction in civil life ; the Negro soldiers were poor ; were ignorant of the power of organization, and on their retirement from the army dropped back into obscurity. The real heroes and leaders of the colored people have been not their soldiers, but those who have been trained for leadership and usefulness in the schools established for them since the war.

Then too it is perhaps fortunate, on the whole, and in keeping with the divine purpose, that the development of the Negroes should be along industrial, educational, and religious lines, rather than as a military or warlike people. Their future seems to be inseparably blended with that of the white people by whom they are surrounded, and an independent career such as they might have if they occupied a country of their own is impossible under existing circumstances. While the success of the experiment of Negro soldiers has had, as has been indicated, a marked and beneficial influence upon the subsequent history of their people, it has not developed in them the military instinct, but has fitted them for more complete absorption and assimilation into our national life, as citizens of the great republic.

NOTE.—Since the above was written, Negro soldiers have achieved great distinction in battle at Santiago, Cuba. As a reward for gallantry the President has promoted a half-dozen enlisted men and made them lieutenants. The Eighth Illinois Infantry, now in Cuba, has only Negro officers from colonel down.

III

EDUCATION OF THE NEGROES

A CHARACTERISTIC of the American people is their love for education. Fostered by public sentiment, there has grown up a magnificent system of schools, maintained by taxation, at an annual expense exceeding one hundred and fifty millions of dollars which, including kindergartens for the very young, primary, intermediate, and grammar schools, high schools, normal schools, and State universities, is being slowly perfected and is contributing very largely toward the education of the masses of the people. It is only a question of time when, chiefly through its agency, the average popular intelligence in America will be higher than that of any other country in the world. This magnificent system is supplemented by great religious institutions and by technical and special schools founded and endowed by public-spirited philanthropists.

It is not invidious to say that the system has

reached a degree of efficiency in the North that is wholly unknown in the South, which is easily explained, chiefly by the fact that it was not established in the South until after the close of the Civil War, 1865. It is also notably true that most of the great universities and colleges of the country, such as Harvard, Brown, Yale, Chicago, Amherst, Williams, Cornell, Rochester; by far the greater number of theological schools, Andover, Newton, Union, Princeton, Rochester, Chicago; and almost all of the great technical schools, are found in the Northern States. Johns Hopkins University, at Baltimore, is hardly an exception, since Baltimore is quite as much a Northern as a Southern city. The great publishing houses are in the North, so also are the most prosperous, widely circulated, and influential newspapers. It would be very surprising, therefore, if it should be maintained that the South is in any respect on the same line with the North in matters of education.

These facts are stated simply with a view of showing their bearing upon the question of the education of the Negroes. While they were held in bondage and treated as chattels, they were, by the very necessity of the system of

Education of the Negroes

slavery, deprived of any educational advantages whatever, except those which came incidentally by reason of their intimate association with their white masters and overseers.

The Pall of Slavery

They were taught to work, became somewhat skilled in the lower forms of industrial occupation, and acquired habits of industry, enforced by the lash, which have been of incalculable service to them. Here and there one by stealth learned to read and write, but the great mass of them could do neither, and were kept in the grossest kind of ignorance. In many of the Southern States it was made a crime to teach a slave his letters. It is not surprising, therefore, that when the exigencies of the war liberated four millions of slaves, made them free men, and cast them upon their own individual resources, they should enter into the competitive struggle of life sadly handicapped.

Even their preachers, in most cases, were grossly ignorant, unable to read a word of the Bible which they were attempting to expound, and there existed among them no class of men who had any proper conception or any suitable preparation for intelligent leadership. Behind the emancipated Negroes, set free by the proclamation of Abraham Lincoln, there stretched a dark and dismal bondage of two hundred and fifty years, unillumined by any except the most feeble rays of light. As they emerged from this dense darkness of ignorance, superstition, and petty vices, they were dazed and terrorized by the new responsibilities of freedom so suddenly thrust upon them. The war had made them free, with little or no preparation for freedom ; the Constitution conferred upon them citizenship, while as yet they had had no training for it and no instruction as to what it meant. Separated by their color and by the prejudice against them, born of slavery, they withdrew from the white congregations, organized churches of their own, and installed as pastors men untrained, uneducated, inexperienced, and incompetent. Thrust into political life with no knowledge of civics, no training or experience in public affairs, they blindly followed the lead either of designing white men or of untrained and incompetent black men, and fell, very naturally, into many a foolish and hurtful act.

Those great steps by which, in the onward march of human events, there has been conceded to the Negro in America his freedom, his citizenship, his manhood, his equality before the law, can never be retraced. The edict of emancipation is as irrevocable as is the Declaration of Independence.

No Step Backward

The rights of full citizenship, including suffrage, once conferred upon a whole race of several millions can never be wholly withdrawn. It may be abridged, modified temporarily, rendered inoperative, but permanently withdrawn or overthrown—never.

A nation can no more escape the consequences of its own action than can the individual: "Whatsoever a man soweth that shall he also reap." The people of America have established upon this continent a republic, a government of the people, having as its cornerstone the equality of man, and the sacred right of the majority to rule. They have by persuasions, entreaties, and by prodigal bestowment of rewards, financial, social, political, peopled the North with millions from Europe, and by force and fraud populated the South with millions from Africa. Upon all these people alike they have conferred the inalienable and priceless boon of American citizenship. They have incorporated all alike into its body politic, into its national life. These hosts are no longer separate peoples—Swedes, English, Irish, French, Germans, Africans—they are Americans.

The rising generation of colored children, for whose education we are concerned, are "native and to the manner born"; sons of freedom who have never known bondage; born into the inherited rights of American citizenship; thousands of them having a just pride in their ancestral history, speaking a common language with us, professing a common Christianity; thoroughly American in spirit, habits, tastes, hopes, and aspirations. They are not aliens, foreigners, strangers. They are part of ourselves. Politically they are "bone of our bone and flesh of our flesh." We must recognize this tremendous fact of vital political relationship which we ourselves have created, and cannot by any possibility unmake.

We may shut our eyes to the fact, but the fact remains; we may attempt to ignore it, but it will not be ignored; we may repent the history that established it, but repentance does not in the very slightest degree modify the fact. The colored branch has been ingrafted into the national stock so that the very life-

Education of the Negroes

blood of the republic flows through its veins. It is impossible now to sever the branch without not only marring the symmetry, but also endangering the very life of the national stock.

The question of the education of the Negroes as a preparation for citizenship, thus thrust upon the public attention, demanded careful thought and prompt and radical treatment. **A Perplexing Problem** From the nature of the case, they themselves were utterly incapable of grappling with the problem; the Southern white people could not be expected to throw to the winds all their traditions and preconceptions, admit at once their former slaves into political fellowship, recognizing them as fellow-citizens entitled, like themselves, to all the rights of citizenship, and especially to that education without which they could neither appreciate the privileges, nor meet the responsibilities of their changed status. That the Negroes have shown as much interest in the cause of education as they have, that they have been as receptive and appreciative of the efforts made in their behalf by others, and that they have made the progress they have made, is a matter for congratulation. That the Southern people—former slaveholders, overwhelmingly defeated in their endeavors to dissolve the Union and establish a confederacy founded on slavery—should accept the situation with as much grace as they have and should be willing to accord to their slaves, torn from them by war, a recognition of their rights as freemen, and that they should provide for them even a rudimentary system of schools maintained by public taxation, the chief burden of which must necessarily fall upon themselves, is creditable to their strong Anglo-Saxon sense.

It is, however, true that the credit for establishing public schools in the South is due chiefly to Northern men who, during the period of reconstruction, secured in the South political pre-eminence ; and it is especially noteworthy that the most influential schools for the Negroes, those which have been the greatest factors in promoting their education, were established by Northern benevolence. The North, in addition to grappling with its own serious problem, has shown a willingness to lend a helping hand to the South and, because it believes profoundly in education, has made large contributions for the establishing of schools for the training of Negro citizens. For this purpose the Friends

Education of the Negroes

have given one million dollars; the Presbyterians, one million, two hundred and fifty thousand; the Baptists, over three million; the Methodists, six million; the Congregationalists, twelve million. Besides this, Mr. Slater contributed one million, and private individuals and churches not named have added largely to the amount. Shaw University, at Raleigh, N. C.; Richmond Theological Seminary; Spelman Seminary, Atlanta University, at Atlanta, Ga.; Roger Williams and Fisk Universities, at Nashville, Tenn.; Leland and Straight Universities, at New Orleans, La.; Bishop College, at Marshall, Texas, and similar schools, have done for Negro education since the war what Harvard, Yale, Dartmouth, and other institutions, wrought in the early history of education in the North.

The present status of Negro education, while encouraging, and possibly creditable in greater or less degree to all parties concerned—to the Southern whites, the Northern philanthropists, and the Negroes themselves—has in it, nevertheless, elements that call for very serious consideration. The Negroes now number not less than eight millions, seven mil-

The Present Status

lions of whom are in the South; in some of the States, notably South Carolina and Mississippi, they outnumber the whites; and in all, their numbers are so great that they must, of necessity, exert a very marked influence upon Southern life, character, and progress. Under the improving conditions, it is reasonable to expect that their natural increase will be certainly as great in the future as in the past. Their number has doubled within a period of thirty years, and it is probable that it will double again within the next thirty, possibly within twenty-five years. Travelers in the South are impressed with the large families which everywhere appear among them.

We must recognize the great fact that they are here to stay, and to rapidly increase in number. Any scheme for their forced colonization would be a wrong second only to that of slavery itself. Humanity would cry out against it. A scheme of voluntary expatriation is chimerical. We may anticipate the emigration of all the sons of Israel from America to Palestine much sooner than that of the sons of Ham to Africa. Missionaries and teachers in increasing numbers will doubtless

They are Here to Stay

Education of the Negroes

go from this favored land to carry the gospel of knowledge and salvation to their countrymen in Africa, and traders and adventurers will follow. Colonies may be planted there, and a century hence thousands may overflow from our fast-filling territory to the more attractive portions of Africa. But the movement of colored people is far more likely to be in the direction of Texas, New Mexico, Arizona, lower California, and even Alaska, than toward Africa. They have been transplanted to American soil and are as thoroughly American in tastes, habits, spirit, as any other element of our population. They are no more Africans than we are Europeans. They are an indestructible part of our nationality.

From whatever point of view we contemplate this great and increasing mass of human beings, whether simply as so many men and women, with human instincts, tastes, temptations, and possibilities; whether as masses of humanity, exerting, of necessity, a tremendous influence upon the social, religious, industrial, and commercial life of the entire South; whether as American citizens, wielding the dreaded power of the ballot and having, by reason of their numbers,

An Urgent Need

accentuated by the doctrine of majority rule, the right to control the political destiny of entire communities, counties, districts, and States; or whether as a vast body of professedly Christian people, Protestant almost entirely, developing a religious life among themselves, and necessarily modifying that of those about them; or as an important constituent element of our national life, destined to overthrow some of our most cherished political theories unless they can be assimilated and rendered thoroughly homogeneous—from whatever point of view we contemplate them, the question of their education is seen to be full of urgency.

Whatever reasons can be advanced for the education of any class of men, can be with reference to the education of this people; whatever can be urged for a perfected public school system for the white children of the North, has equal significance in behalf of a perfected public school system for the Negro children of the South. There is no argument for the endowment and equipment of great institutions of learning, colleges, theological seminaries, technical schools, for the favored white children of the North, that

Diversified Schools

Education of the Negroes

would not have probably equal weight in behalf of establishing similar institutions for the black children of the South :—Kindergartens for the little ones, to awaken and train their senses, develop their consciences, and start them in a career of quickening growth and development ; elementary schools, to give them the mastery of the instruments of learning—reading, writing, spelling, arithmetic—and to bring them into touch with the educational forces of the day ; industrial education, to fit them to earn an honest living, and especially to show them the vast possibilities of improved and diversified industries that lie everywhere about them in the as yet undeveloped sunny Southland ; business schools, to fit them for the ordinary pursuits of commercial life ; normal schools, to provide for them competent teachers capable of training those committed to their care, according to philosophical principles and modern approved methods ; colleges, to furnish them with an all-around intellectual development, to open to them vistas into untrodden fields of learning, to fit them for independent investigation, to arouse within them consciousness of power, and to awaken aspirations after worthy achievements and conquests in all the varied departments of mental activity; professional schools—medical, legal, and theological, to train a body of men competent for the important duties and responsibilities that rest upon the pastor, the physician, and the legal adviser; technical schools, to develop among them architects, artists, engineers, master-mechanics, superintendents of mines, overseers of mills, and men capable of leading their people in the fierce competition that must grow in intensity as the resources of the South are developed, and as the expected immigration from the North increases in volume.

If the question is raised, what sort of schools are required for them? we answer, schools modeled after those of like grade established for white people. There are required the same qualifications in the teachers, the same text-books, the same course of study, the same kinds of discipline that are found in similar institutions. There seems to be no point in the equipment or general management of these institutions where they can diverge safely from those which the history of education has shown to be most desirable

Culture is Colorless

Education of the Negroes

and best adapted to their purpose. The grounds, buildings, furniture, libraries, text-books, apparatus, endowments of a Negro school in Georgia, do not differ in any respect from the equipment of a similar institution for a white school in Massachusetts.

The fundamental endowments of the human mind—the five senses of sight, touch, taste, smell, and hearing; the memory, imagination, and the reasoning powers; the desire for wealth, power, knowledge; the conscience—are essentially the same in every human being; they are the constituent elements of the soul; they belong in common to Negroes and to Caucasians.

The chief aim of culture is the development of these fundamental faculties. Education aims to evolve power, capacity. The law of development of the senses, the desires, the reasoning powers, or the moral nature, are the same for all races. They all grow by use; they are trained by exercise; are called into activity by methods and means which are alike for all.

The principal agent for the unfolding of mental power is knowledge—knowledge of language, science, philosophy, mathematics, history, etc. Knowledge is one. Mathematics knows nothing of race, color, or condition; philosophy and history are utterly indifferent to the color of the skin of the student who consults them; the spelling book, the dictionary, and the encyclopædia tell the same story to every class of inquirers. There is not one multiplication table for the whites and another for the blacks; the Ten Commandments were not published for one fragment of the human race.

The chief outcome of culture is character; self-respect; love of the true, the beautiful, and the good; firmness of will; sensitiveness of conscience; refinement of taste. Character is a quality of the soul and independent of the physical features. Indians, Negroes, half-breeds, whites, are alike amenable to the immutable laws by which men are judged, and require, in their process of preparation to meet these demands, the same course of training.

In this country the destiny of men and women is not determined by any fixed lines; more and more there is public recognition of talent, preparation, fitness, merit. Breadth of opportunity should have a corresponding breadth of preparation. The old chasm that separated the free and the slave has been—not bridged over, but filled up by the costly *débris* of a civil war. In the eye of the law all American citizens are equal; preparation for American citizenship must take this great fact into consideration.

God, who made of one blood all nations of men, looks not upon the color of the skin or the texture of the hair, but upon the quality of the soul. Christian culture, which seeks to fit men and women for service in the kingdom of God and for participation in the joys of heaven, must build its foundations, not upon the accident of birth, but upon the indestructible image of God which every soul bears within itself. Heaven is not divided into compartments; it recognizes neither caste nor color.

The human soul is God's masterpiece. To develop it, train it, awaken all its energies, prepare it for the broadest sphere of usefulness and the noblest plane of activity, is one of life's highest privileges; the teacher is God's co-worker. The spirit, method, and means of education should correspond to the dignity of the work to be done.

How these various institutions are to be provided is the serious, practical question that meets every man who has any official relation to it. Will the Southern States appreciate the importance of the situation and tax themselves sufficiently to maintain for all the colored people an adequate, efficient system of public schools? Their own self-interest demands it, but it is possible they may not recognize this. Will the Negroes themselves appreciate the peril that confronts them, and recognize that they are at the "parting of the ways," where they can, on the one hand, settle down to a position of hopeless, indifferent degradation and contempt, disgraceful to themselves, harmful to their neighbors, and possibly disastrous to free institutions and the cause of human liberty; or, on the other hand, where, by self-sacrifice, persistence, and zeal, they may insist that their children shall be educated, that they shall have an equipment for life equal in all respects to that enjoyed by their white competitors, that they will be satisfied with nothing less than an all-around and thorough training, and that they will be willing to pay the cost of it, so far as lies in their power? Would they might do so.

Who will Provide Schools?

Education of the Negroes

In addition to paying taxes to maintain public schools, they are doing what they can to establish and support higher Christian schools, and are showing a spirit of zeal and sacrifice to secure the proper education of their children ; but they are distressingly poor. Their energies are, and must be for a long time to come, largely absorbed in the struggle for existence. To improve their condition by the purchase of property and the erection of homes will tax them severely. In their present condition it is a great strain upon them to meet the current expenses of their churches and pay their taxes. Those of them who are attempting to give their children an academic or collegiate education, find the cost very heavy. It cannot be expected that a people, just emerging from slavery, with its attendant barbarism, should have any but the most crude ideas relating to education. They cannot be expected to appreciate the incalculable advantage to their children of institutions of higher learning. They are doing something, and indeed many of them are making great sacrifices for these institutions, but unless they can have help, speedy, generous help from the North,

The Negroes are Poor

their efforts to secure for their children the education which their circumstances imperatively demand must end in failure.

Will the philanthropists in the North see in the emancipation of the slaves clear indications of the Providence of God and realize what is involved for human liberty, for republican institutions, for Christianity, for civilization itself, in the thorough education of the masses of Negro American citizens?

A Call to Philanthropists

This is a crisis in the history of the colored people. They are on trial. They have been faithful servants in bondage, patient sufferers in tribulation, brave soldiers on the battlefield. Elevated suddenly to the exalted plane of freedom, citizenship, manhood, will they prove equal to the demands of the hour? Are they hopelessly inferior to the white race? Are they fit only for servitude? Are they doomed to degradation? Is all Africa to be abandoned to barbarism?

Surely we ought not to expect them to vie with their white competitors in the great race without equal advantages. For centuries we have had the accumulated treasures of knowledge, the inherited glories of literature, the

Education of the Negroes

inspiration of great leaders in science and philosophy, and the invaluable help of countless schools of learning.

We ask for them what we have had ourselves. Give them a fair chance; open to them the school, the academy, the college, the university; call out their latent talent; give them time for development of great preachers, lawyers, physicians, philosophers, scientists, and statesmen, as well as captains of industry, master workmen, successful farmers, and skillful mechanics. Africa has need of them. Notwithstanding the teeming millions already there, there is room for multitudes of others from here who will carry with them the seeds of a new civilization. Not in our day, but in the future, largely through the instrumentality of educated Christian Negro Americans, there is to be doubtless are generation of the Dark Continent. It will be a new and glorious chapter in the history of humanity.

IV

THE HIGHER EDUCATION OF NEGRO WOMEN

BEFORE entering upon the discussion of this theme it may be well to prepare the way by a few simple definitions. Education is a somewhat vague term, and may mean much or little, according to the intent of him who uses it. The new-born babe is simply a bundle of possibilities. If normally constituted, it may develop a strong, healthy, vigorous body, an active mind, and a sound moral and religious nature. Left to itself absolutely, it will necessarily perish, the young of the human species being among the most helpless of God's creatures and the most dependent upon parental care. If it is provided with food, raiment, shelter, and association with others, it will, in process of time, acquire a certain degree of physical, intellectual, and moral development.

There is a sense in which this natural growth may be called education. "We are born weak, we need strength; we are born destitute

The Higher Education of Negro Women

of all things, we need assistance; we are born stupid, we need judgment. All that we have not at our birth, and that we need when grown up, is given us by education." Ordinarily, however, when we use the term education we mean by it that special process of development of mind and body and acquisition of knowledge which are the result either of conscious effort on the part of the child or of instruction and training given by others. When the mother is teaching the child to talk, she is training it in language; when she teaches it to count, she is educating it in mathematics; when she tells it the names and habits of the dooryard fowls or the domestic animals, she is teaching it zoölogy; when she teaches it the names and uses of its own hands, eyes, etc., it is a lesson in physiology; when she describes the flowers that bloom in the garden, she is instructing it in botany; when she takes it with her on her walks to her neighbors, and points out to it the names and direction of places, she is instructing it in geography; when she points out sun and moon and stars, she is educating it in astronomy; when she reproves it for misconduct, rewards it for good behavior, and inculcates into its young mind principles of conduct, she is instructing it in morals; when she tells it of the great God above us, and of the love of Christ for us, she is training it in theology; when she directs its energies in useful ways, teaching it to perform little acts of service about the house, she is giving to it industrial education. A child's first lessons in handling the needle, sweeping the floor, whittling a stick, washing dishes, chopping wood, running a sewing machine, comprise the rudiments of manual training. In these rudimentary and homely efforts are found all the elements involved in the science and practice of education; these are the beginnings of a process which differs only in degree, from the time it begins in the mother's arms until it culminates in the higher classes in the university. It is a process of communicating knowledge, imparting impulses, directing energies, controlling activities, developing character.

When the child enters school it passes from one grade of instruction to another, from the acquisition of one class of facts to that of another class, from informal to formal instruction; from isolated training to class or associated training; from parental tuition to the instruction and discipline of a teacher; from

The Higher Education of Negro Women

the study of nature to the study of books. There is no necessarily radical change either of topics or methods; and it still studies the language, geography, arithmetic, botany, zoölogy, etc., which have already engaged its attention in its mother's arms or at her side. Happy is the child whose earliest years have been blessed with careful, loving, intelligent, parental training, and who passes from the home into the school with a desire for knowledge and with such a foundation laid as will enable it to profit in the highest degree by the enlarged advantages which the school affords.

It is by no means easy to draw a sharp line through this process of education which shall separate it into two clearly discriminated degrees, one of which we may call the lower education and the other higher education. **Higher and Lower** In the sense of being fundamental and important, it may be said, paradoxically, that the lowest is the highest; and, since the entire future development of the soul depends so largely upon the start the child receives in its earliest years, the greatest significance attaches to the methods employed and the results attained during the first few years of its life.

The foundations of the attainments in knowledge, discipline, and power are laid while the child is still young, and before it has entered upon that which we commonly call the higher studies. For the purposes of convenience, we are accustomed to apply the term "secondary" education to all those processes and results characteristic of education prior to the student's entering upon a full college course of study; by higher education we usually mean that which is comprised within a college or university course. When the question is asked, Shall women have a higher education? we generally mean by it, Shall they go to college and shall they pursue university studies? Higher education simply means better education, better mental discipline, a stronger grasp of fundamental principles, a broader outlook, a clearer judgment, a firmer will; more knowledge, more power, a nobler character.

It is now well-nigh universally conceded by all who are interested in and acquainted with the present condition of the colored people, that the girls and young women ought to have a common-school education. That is, that they should be able to read the English language with fluency and intelligence, to spell

The Higher Education of Negro Women

correctly, to write legibly and with a fair degree of facility, so as to express themselves intelligibly; that they should be acquainted with the principles of arithmetic, know something of geography and history, and have, at least, a rudimentary knowledge of physiology, botany, chemistry, and physics. There is no difference of opinion either regarding the desirability of their special training in the performance of household duties, or their preparation for the responsible position of trained nurses, or in such other lines of industrial acquirements as will fit them to earn an independent livelihood. It is also generally conceded that the time has now come when the average attainment among the colored women calls for a much more thorough training and a higher degree of culture than was called for ten years ago. There is a sense in which this secondary or academic work is a high education; that is, it is higher or more advanced than has been given heretofore. But this is not the higher education for which I now plead.

In my judgment it is wise that the opportunity should be afforded to these young women to pursue college studies, to secure those advantages of higher education which are offered to white girls in the best organized colleges and universities in the country.

Shall Negro Women Go to College? White women are now freely admitted, not only to Smith, Wellesley, Vassar, and other women's colleges, where the curriculum of study is as high, as thorough, as in men's colleges of the same grade, but they are likewise admitted on terms of intellectual equality to the classes in many of the best equipped colleges and universities of the country, such as Michigan and Chicago Universities. Without going into an elaborate discussion of the subject, I will instance three reasons, somewhat comprehensive, which to my mind are conclusive arguments for offering to the young Negro women of the present day the opportunities for acquiring this higher education.

1. The first is because they are women. The worthiest conceivable outcome of education is the development of the soul. Education properly conducted results in training all the powers to their greatest and healthiest activity. The educated person is he who is able to make the best use of his

A Completed Womanhood

The Higher Education of Negro Women

powers of observation, in the acquisition, at first hand, of elementary knowledge of nature; the educated eye sees, the educated ear hears, the educated palate tastes, the educated nose smells, and the educated hand touches as the uneducated cannot, and thus makes it possible for the educated soul to enjoy a boundless range of rich experiences to which the uneducated soul is a stranger. All the glories of the oratorio are in germ in training of the ear, and all the boundless pleasures of form and color, architecture, painting, sculpture, landscape, are patent to the eye trained to see them; likewise the reasoning powers, analysis, comparison, inference, judgment, reach their grandest development only through the process of education. Man is a rational animal; reasoning is one of his distinctive characteristics; he fulfills his position in the scale of being in proportion as he is in full possession of his reasoning faculties; whatever promotes the development of his mental powers adds to his happiness and his dignity; the same is true in a certain degree of the development of his memory, his imagination, his power of expression, and also of his moral nature. The glory of the elm tree is in the strength of its trunk and its wide-spreading, graceful branches; it does not attain its true dignity until it is fully grown. The glory of the human soul is in the full stature and vigor of all its powers; so long as any of these are undeveloped, it falls short of its true dignity. Education is the process by which these powers are developed, and higher education is simply the higher degree of activity, exercise, growth, attainment, development. The fact that an elm tree is an elm tree entitles it to whatever of soil, sunshine, and opportunity will secure for it the completest unfolding of all the possibilities of its nature which lie wrapped up in the tiny seed. So too, the fact that a colored woman is a woman, made in the image of God, bearing his likeness, capable of high attainments, is a sufficient reason why she should have the opportunity, at least, of bringing her powers to their normal unfolding.

A generation ago the colored women of the South were slaves, chattels, without personality; to-day they are free, and in the enjoyment of many of the privileges of liberty. They are recognized as women, who, by virtue of their womanhood, are entitled to the protection of the laws and the shield of public

The Higher Education of Negro Women

opinion. By the slow process of education there is being evolved among them a class of women having enlarged capacity for culture, a truer self-consciousness, a keener sensitiveness, purer and loftier aspirations, and greater possibilities of achievement, a new and improved type of womanhood, destined by their influence upon their race to mark a new era in its history.

The noblest thing in nature is man. The noblest thing in man is mind. The highest attainments of mind are conditioned on education. There is no sex in culture. The mind is the woman, and soul culture is woman's birthright because she is a woman.

> He that made us with such large discourse,
> Looking before and after, gave us not
> That capability and godlike reason
> To rust in us unused.

2. I urge as a subordinate reason why colored women should have the opportunity of higher education, the fact that in most cases they are to be wives. The home is at once the humblest, the highest, and the holiest place on earth. It is there that we

The Responsibilities of Wifehood

come into the most intimate relations with each other. It is there that character is most severely tested; it is there that the experiences of life are most concentrated; it is there that character is most fully developed; and it is there where is heard the loudest and most imperious call for all the help that knowledge, training, and experience can render. A happy home, where order, intelligence, thrift, and love reign, is a miniature heaven on earth. In such an atmosphere men and women enjoy together the sweetest experiences of living, are refreshed, strengthened, and equipped for the burdens, toils, and conflicts of life. The happy home takes from life's disappointments and sorrows their keenest sting, and gives to existence its truest and holiest significance.

The home is what the wife makes it. She reigns there as sovereign; its atmosphere is a reflection of her own mind. If she is a woman of intelligence, taste, tact, resources, character, she can make the rudest cabin seem a palace and the humblest home an Eden. All her defects in mental and moral equipment will express themselves in some bitter fashion in the daily life of the home. How dependent upon the wife the husband is none know so well

The Higher Education of Negro Women

as he who has been blessed with one whose higher education has fitted her for the noble functions of her position.

It hardly need to be said that the children carry through all subsequent life the impress made upon them in their earliest years by the mother. It is her molding and guid- **The Mother's Impress** ing hand which, more than any other agency, shapes their destiny. Their future is in her keeping. If she herself has enjoyed the advantages of a liberal education, and has acquired thereby that knowledge, skill, self-discipline, power of directive energy, high ideals of life, and practical common sense that ought to come from college training, she will be able out of the fullness of her own life to impart to her children such impulses, principles, methods, tastes, and habits, as will secure for them a larger place in life's enjoyments and duties than they otherwise could possibly occupy. If we desire to improve the condition of the race, purify our homes, renovate society, promote the highest public welfare, impart new energy and fidelity to the church, and to secure the best results to human civilization, we must seek to promote the education of the wives and mothers. If the reservoir is sweet, all the faucets in the city will send forth pure water.

3. A third reason for the higher education of colored women is, that such education fits them for work. Life is activity; we are called upon to labor; none are exempt. Colored women are no exception to the rule. They are born neither to leisure nor to laziness, but because they are women, and especially because they are colored women, perhaps, they are called to a life of service. Not all of them are to be servants, as we commonly use that term, and spend their days in the kitchen, the laundry, and the nursery; but even if this were the case, higher education would be very helpful to them in this sphere of life.

Preparation for Work

The suffering, the annoyances, the losses of time, to say nothing of the diseases and death occasioned by unintelligent service in our homes would be appalling if merely stated. There is a science of housekeeping and a philosophy of cooking, and our homes will never be what they ought to be until our cooks are philosophers and our housekeepers are scientists.

There is among the colored people, both in

The Higher Education of Negro Women

America and in Africa, a wide-open door for the highest sort of missionary service, which can be rendered most effectively by colored women of strong character and liberal culture. Such women will have an influence upon the home life, the religious culture and activities of the colored people, limited only by their fitness for their work. A thousand such women, distributed throughout the churches of the South, would slowly but surely lift the general average of piety, morality, intelligence, and character of the whole mass.

But passing now to the wide domain of teaching, where so many colored women will find their life-work, we are confronted at once with the **Teaching** fact that we are committing to them, in a very large measure, the destiny of the Afro-Americans of this country. The eight millions of that race are destined, within another century, to become probably not less than fifty millions, and to exert an enormous influence in the development of our national life. The vast multitudes of their children will receive what education they get almost exclusively at the hands of colored women school teachers. The stream can rise no higher than its source; if these women are ignorant and unqualified, the schools which they teach will be of low grade, and the instruction which they impart and the characteristics they develop will be accordingly dwarfed and unsymmetrical. Heretofore the efforts of philanthropists and statesmen who have taken cognizance of this need for competent colored teachers, have been directed chiefly toward providing them with a rudimentary normal training which has consisted to a very large degree, in giving them a common school education. It has been rightly estimated that in order to teach the Three R's the colored women need themselves to be taught, and very little has been attempted beyond the simplest forms of instruction. We are now entering upon a second stage of this process of preparing school teachers, by giving them the elements of pedagogical training; they are taught something of psychology, something of school management, something of the history of education, a little of the philosophy of teaching. This professional work is yet in its earliest stages, and will require some years for its complete evolution. That there is the same necessity for strictly professional, normal school education among the colored people of

The Higher Education of Negro Women

the South that there is among the white people of the North, where so much has been done in this direction, hardly needs argument.

Within a comparatively few years great progress has been made in public sentiment as to the need of a college training as the basis for normal professional training. Accuracy of information in the common school branches, breadth of general knowledge, maturity of mind, discipline of mental power, and that indescribable something which we call culture, are recognized as being, if not absolutely essential to him who would make the most of a normal school course, as at least giving to the normal school graduate a preparation for a grade of work entirely beyond the reach of those who have been denied the privilege of college education. Teaching is one of the most exalted and dignified among human vocations. It is the privilege of the teacher to develop character, and he does this largely by imparting to the pupil something of his own inner life. The higher and the richer his life, the more inexhaustible his own resources, the greater and grander will be the results of his work.

It is not extravagant to say that there is a

present demand, far outrunning the supply, for college-bred women as teachers in the colored schools, public and private. Unless this want can be supplied, these schools will lack the vitality, vigor, and virtue so essential to their highest success. No work for the colored people exceeds in urgency and importance that of training, in the best possible way, a select class of women who shall be fully competent to take their places in the colleges, academies, high schools, grammar schools, and normal schools, where at present so many colored women are engaged in attempting to do a work for which they have had no adequate preparation.

We are about to enter upon the twentieth century of the Christian era. The human race is making great progress upward, and in nothing is this progress more marked than in the place it accords to women. Their spheres of activity have been enlarged and multiplied, and to-day the women, especially in America, are making their influence felt more and more, not only in the home, but in society, in the church, and in all great intellectual, social, missionary, and religious activi-

The Twentieth Century

The Higher Education of Negro Women

ties. The education of women ought to keep pace with their opportunities. Privilege and power should go together. Higher education is coming to be universally recognized as one of the essential elements that shall prepare women both for the enjoyment of all the privileges that the age offers to them and for the performance of the multiplied duties that it exacts from them. While the mass of women, both white and colored, are undoubtedly destined for many years to come to grow up in comparative ignorance, with limited education, and with little fitness either to enjoy or to do, there is an increasing recognition of the necessity of offering to all those who will avail themselves of the opportunities, wider and wider privileges for study. We only ask for the colored women that they shall share in this general progress of the race. We believe that the same considerations which justify any systematic attempt to develop the minds of the young through any lower stage, prove the desirability of offering to the few the opportunity for continuing the process through its higher stages. The spelling-book is the key to knowledge. If we give the key to the colored woman, we do not see why we should not offer her the privilege of using it to unlock whatever treasure-house of learning she wishes to explore.

These three reasons, then, because they are Women, because most of them will be Wives, because all of them will be Workers, seem to me to be ample justification for the statement that colored women ought to have the advantages of the higher or college education.

V

RELIGIOUS LIFE AMONG THE NEGROES

The African contingent of American life presents many interesting questions in sociology, among the most important being that of the development of the religious life. In addition to the knowledge gained by personal observation, extending through many years,—including experience as an officer of colored troops,—supplemented by information gleaned from books and other sources, I have recently addressed a series of questions to a number of men, white and black, Northern and Southern, who have had exceptional opportunities for observation, and shall now attempt, as far as such a thing is practicable, to state a few generalizations, fully realizing how imperfect the sketch must be.

The American Negroes comprise several distinct classes. First, those who were imported into this country from Africa; second, those born in America of African parentage; third, the full-blood African born in this country, whose parents were likewise natives of America; fourth, the mixed race, varying from those who have merely a suggestion of white blood, to those who have only a trace of Negro blood left. The imported Africans, brought here in slaveships, were heathen, grossly ignorant, full of superstition, and having only the crudest conception of religion. These poor creatures, emerging from African barbarism into American bondage, did not offer a very promising field for the development of a pure and intelligent Christianity, for, though the soil was rich enough, it hardly seemed adapted to such a harvest. African nature is simply human nature bound in black—"God's image carved in ebony"—but neither an African barbarian nor a Negro slave is the ideal of an enlightened Christian.

There are minor differences which differentiate the African from the Caucasian, and yet in essential elements they are alike. They are both human. Many of the differences are traceable to environment. The conditions of life which surrounded them in Africa were widely different from those which confronted them in their new home in the United States. There was unbroken heathenism of a very de-

Religious Life Among the Negroes

graded type; here they were surrounded on all sides by a Christian civilization, with its schools, churches, and the other fruits and agencies of progress, and the white men to whom slavery introduced them were easily recognized as vastly superior to the black men in Africa with whom they had formerly associated. In due course of time Christianity made very considerable progress among them. Many of them received faithful Christian instruction in the homes of their masters, and large numbers were converted by the earnest preaching of white pastors. They were cordially welcomed at least to the galleries and back seats in white churches, and no inconsiderable number of them were admitted into full membership, where they enjoyed practically the same religious instruction. But, of course, they were neither able to receive it in the same way that it was received by their more cultivated white friends, nor to embody their religious aspirations in order and form with any great degree of freedom, although occasionally some of those who exhibited extraordinary aptitudes were allowed to devote a considerable portion of their time to preaching.

Speaking in general terms of the eight million

Negroes in this country at the present time, I think it is safe to say that in the main, subject to local modifications, their religious status may be approximately characterized in the following statements:

An unusually large proportion of them are professing Christians. It is reported that more than one million six hundred thousand of their adults are communicants in regular Baptist churches, while more than another million are enrolled in the Methodist churches; besides these, other thousands are found in connection with other evangelical denominations. The progress of Christianity among them since the war has been phenomenal, unsurpassed, if equaled at any time during the history of Christian missions.

They have shown a remarkable degree of liberality in contributing toward religious purposes. Notwithstanding their poverty and the discouraging circumstances surrounding them, they have, in addition to the ordinary expenses of maintaining religious worship, including pastors' salaries, contributed probably not less than ten million dollars for the erection of meeting houses. Some of these buildings are large, costly, convenient, and attractive.

Religious Life Among the Negroes

They have done remarkably well, considering all the circumstances, in the matter of educational, missionary, charitable, and philanthropic work, many of their religious institutions of learning being managed by Negro Boards of trustees, taught by Negro teachers, and supported largely or entirely by themselves. They are also represented on the Boards and in the faculties of the schools maintained for them by Northern benevolence. The aggregate amount which they pay annually toward the education of their children in Christian institutions is a very considerable sum. They have their local, State, and national educational and missionary organizations, and are year by year making progress in the art of organization and administration. While they have very much yet to learn in the matter of systematizing their beneficence, of keeping and rendering accurate accounts of money received and disbursed, they are apt learners and are making good progress. They edit and publish numerous religious periodicals, some of them evincing vigor, independence, and no little ability. They have not produced any noteworthy books.

Religious life among them is still characterized by a predominance of the emotional element. They are fond of music, and singing constitutes an important part of their worship. Those who have never heard the unrestrained outburst of melody in a Negro congregation, singing under religious excitement, cannot understand the completeness with which a soul may empty itself in song. The preaching which affects them most powerfully is that which deals in vivid description and appeals to their imaginations. Strong statement, frequent repetition, apt illustration, are much more forceful to their understanding than severely logical appeals.

The divorcement between religion and morality is still painfully apparent among many Negro Christians, but several of my correspondents insist that it does not exist to a greater degree than it does among white people of a similar grade of culture. From a somewhat wide observation, I am strongly inclined to the opinion that this judgment is just. When we reflect that lynching in the South and the suppression of the ballot by fraud, intimidation, or violence are catalogued among the vices chargeable to the whites and not to the Negro; when we recall the fact that in almost all cases the mixed bloods call the white man father; and

Religious Life Among the Negroes

we also remember that in the North large numbers of white saloon keepers and multitudes of criminals in our prisons are church-members, we are obliged to broaden our generalization when we attempt to characterize Negro religion as lacking in morality.

It is, I believe, the universal testimony of all well-informed persons, that the type of piety among the Negroes generally is slowly and steadily improving. It is becoming more intelligent, more moral; less superstitious, less emotional, and conforms more and more fully to the New Testament ideal.

Assuming now for a moment, tentatively and diffidently, the *rôle* of a prophet, I venture to suggest that in another half-century, when the Negro population of this country will number from twenty-five to thirty millions, their religious life will be characterized chiefly by the following marks : Their form of church government will be largely congregational, with special emphasis upon the independence of the churches, tempered by some stress upon the power and authority of the pastor ; their mode of worship will throw off that which is now grotesque and offensive to refined taste, while retaining as peculiarly its own an especial warmth of feeling. It will be a religion of the heart rather than of the head. While education will make its impress both upon the pulpit and upon the pew, it will develop, not intellectualism, but a softened, chastened, intelligent emotionalism. Faith, while not wholly discarding philosophy, will vindicate itself as the highest expression of feeling. While not sternly and severely ethical, their religious life will be moral and be marked by approaching conformity not only to the Ten Commandments, but to the ethical teachings of the Sermon on the Mount. Discarding the allurements of æsthetic and gorgeous ritualism, the Negroes will cultivate and bring to a high state of development pulpit oratory and sacred music. Negro religion will add to its other graces the grace of liberality, pouring its contributions freely into missionary, philanthropic, and charitable channels.

VI

NEGROPHOBIA

RACE antipathies are universal. The German dislikes the Frenchman ; the Frenchman has an antipathy for the Spaniard ; the Irish and the English are separated not only by the channel, but also by race prejudice. To the ancient Greeks all other people were barbarians, while the Jews characterized the rest of mankind as Gentiles, pronouncing the word with a frown and injecting into it a lofty scorn. It is frequently the case that two races of people will live side by side, generation after generation, each preserving its own language, manners, and customs, cherishing its own *hauteur*, looking with disdain upon even the virtues of its neighbor. It is indeed rare that separate and distinct peoples ever completely blend into one nationality. The persistence of the Anglo-Saxon, the Scotch, the Irish, and the Welsh types of character, existing side by side for centuries, under a common government, is a case in point.

The Negro in America

In America, where there is a greater blending of different peoples than has ever occurred before, the process of assimilation and unification has gone on with increasing rapidity, and were it not for the tides of immigration emptying upon our shores, year by year, vast numbers from the different nations of the old world, the day might be predicted with some degree of certainty when the people of the United States would be substantially one, and when the lines that now separate them into national classes—Germans, Irish, Scandinavians, Poles, Russians, Americans—would disappear. The forces at work, a common language, the public schools, the newspapers, free intercourse, the leveling process of republican institutions, are well-nigh irresistible, and are serving to destroy, except as a reminiscence and a bit of race sentiment, all distinctions based upon previous nationality. The third generation is American and divides into classes along other and artificial lines,—wealth, culture, occupation,—and not upon those of race.

National Assimilation

One of the marked exceptions to this process which attracts the attention of every student of American life, is the persistence of the race

Negrophobia

line that separates the Negro from the Caucasian. While this statement is subject to slight modifications, it is true as a general proposition that the Negroes, or as they are commonly called, the colored people, are a class by themselves, who are separated from others by a well-known, impassable gulf. Out of a total population of about seventy millions, there are, approximately, eight millions who are classed as Negroes, and though there is a large illicit mixture of Caucasian blood, they are regarded not as Americans simply, but as Negroes. There is a well-marked antipathy to them; sometimes this is very slight, indeed, scarcely perceptible, and in individual cases it disappears. But, speaking in general terms, there exists on the part of the Caucasian element of American life a strong, deeply seated prejudice against the Negro; he is looked upon as an inferior, treated as an alien, and is denied the privileges that are freely accorded to others. There is a marked discrimination against the Negroes as Negroes.

A Notable Exception

It would not be fair to say that they are hated, that there exists well-defined Negrophobia among us, as characteristic of our national life; and yet in some portions of the country the unreasoning and unjust dislike amounts practically to a disease, and is not inaptly described as Negrophobia. This dislike shows itself primarily, and in its most marked form, in social ostracism. Negroes are practically banished from the society of the Caucasian. While intermarriage between all other constituent elements of the American people is common and excites no comment (the Chinese scarcely offer an exception to this), intermarriage on the part of the Negroes with white people is tabooed. Such alliances serve to alienate from the white race, in some States the law prohibiting them and setting the seal of illegitimacy upon the offspring. There is practically no social intermingling of the races; Negroes are not invited to social entertainments by white people, and only in exceptional cases are they allowed to sit at the same table. They do not frequent the same hotels nor occupy the same boarding-houses; ordinarily they do not live in the same quarter of the city occupied by white people. Even in the North the sale of a house to a Negro in a fashionable part of a city would probably cause an immediate decline

Negrophobia

in the price of real estate in that section. In many of the Northern cities there are spots known as "Little Africa," occupied chiefly by Negroes, with a sprinkling of the lower grade of whites. Everywhere throughout the South, and generally throughout the North, they have their separate churches, and are seldom seen in any considerable numbers in white congregations; in theatres and other places of entertainment, frequently in the North and universally in the South, they are separated from other spectators.

There are two curious features about this race antipathy between the Caucasian and the African; one is, that it is confined almost exclusively to the Caucasian. Negroes manifest, in most cases, a good deal of affection for the white people, and are very ready to accept service of any sort which brings them into relationship with them. As house servants, body servants, nurses, field hands, porters, waiters, they are faithful, docile, affectionate, and in extreme cases almost servile. It is true that there has been since the war an increasing disposition, on the part of ambitious colored men, "to draw the color line," and to insist, partly, it is to be feared, for selfish purposes, that all positions of honor and profit, especially in the Negro schools, shall be filled by Negroes, to the exclusion of even more competent white people.

The other fact is, that the antipathy of the white man against the Negro is, apparently, chiefly a matter of caste and culture, and not a native instinct. **Caste and Culture** In the days of slavery, white and colored children mingled together in the most unrestrained freedom, and they do so still. It was very common for the master and the mistress of the plantation to commit their children, while infants, to the care of black nurses, who had the entire oversight of them and showed them the most tender affection. The children reciprocated this affection, and oftentimes seemed to cherish a stronger love for their black nurses than they did for their white mothers. It is very common even now to hear eminent Southern men, publicly and privately, speak rather boastingly of their affection for their "black mammy." Blood-blending of the races in the South, fostered by slavery—and still prevalent in spite of the restrictions of liberty which recognize the black man as the natural protector of his family—would, apparently, in the course of time, result in complete amalgamation if left to the operation of natural laws.

While at the North Negroes are admitted to the public schools, colleges, and universities, on terms of equality with other students, it is not so at the South, where the doors of the higher institutions patronized by the whites are locked and barred against the entrance of any person, however worthy, in whose veins there is a suspicion of colored blood. **Color Line in Schools** The public schools are divided into two distinct classes, one for the whites and one for the Negroes; and even in sparsely settled rural districts, where it is difficult to maintain free schools, this expensive and arbitrary distinction is kept up. In some of the Southern States separate coaches on the railroad trains are set apart for them, and though they pay the same fare and may be well dressed, intelligent, virtuous, clean, polite, sensitive, they are obliged to accept inferior accommodations, and are often subjected to indignities and inconvenience on account of their color.

The prejudice against the Negro shows itself

in his practical exclusion from most of the desirable positions in business. He may be a porter on a train, but not a conductor; a fireman, possibly, but not an engineer; he may run a barber shop, but not be a master carpenter; he may drive a hack or keep a saloon, but he must not be a merchant; he may be a watchman in a bank, but he cannot be a bookkeeper or cashier. Of course there are exceptions to what is here said, but the general statement remains true, that the Negroes are debarred from active participation in the most desirable and remunerative forms of industry and of business.

A notable exception to this general rule is found in their employment by the government in responsible positions under the Civil Service rules. In many of the departments at Washington there are Negro men and women who have secured their places by competitive examination; even here, however, it is true that color serves as a bar to appointment, and not unfrequently, it is said, is an occasion for dismissal.

While the Negro is made a citizen by the United States Constitution, and is entitled to all the rights and privileges attaching to citizenship, and while the theory of the republican

Negrophobia

Practically Disfranchised

government is the right of every legally qualified voter to participate in political affairs, to vote and be voted for, and while the fundamental element that underlies American institutions is the right of the majority to rule, the fact remains as a curious anomaly, that, practically, he is disfranchised in a considerable portion of the South. The un-American dictum which embodies the political philosophy that results in his practical disfranchisement in many portions of the country is, "This is a white man's government," which is a plain and explicit repudiation of the Constitution, and a revolutionary denial of republicanism. It is political Negrophobia, the denial to a whole class of people, simply on the ground of color, of the rights and privileges incident to manhood, and guaranteed by the most august political document in the world. It is not meant here that Negroes are not allowed to vote in some places, nor that in certain localities they are not even elected to office. There is probably an improving public sentiment at the South, as a whole, in regard to their political rights; nevertheless, the fact remains as stated, that by reason of race prejudice they suffer restriction, limitation, and injustice in political matters which are not suffered by any other class of American citizens.

Dislike of the Negroes because they are Negroes manifests itself also in certain portions of the country in acts of injustice. It is said, and believed, that in many cases they are convicted and punished for offenses against the law, where white men would be either acquitted or more lightly punished. In some cases the presumption appears to be, not that they are innocent until proven guilty, but that they are guilty as charged unless they can establish their innocence. This is doubtless an extreme statement, and yet its accuracy is vouched for. The numerous cases of lynching, putting men to death without trial by judge or jury, oftentimes on the mere suspicion of crime, is, perhaps, the most startling manifestation of the disease of Negrophobia which has thus far shown itself. Doubtless there are cases that are very aggravating, where crimes of great enormity and brutality have been committed and where the slow and sometimes tedious processes of law are very trying to the public patience; nevertheless, the fact seems

Injustice

to be established beyond question that Negroes have suffered from lawlessness out of all proportion to the crimes committed, and far beyond any other class of citizens.

Every man of whatever condition when accused of crime is entitled to a fair trial. No man should be hung on suspicion.

Among the unhappy results flowing from this unreasoning prejudice—a prejudice that voices itself in such opprobrious epithets as "niggers," "darkies," "coons," "bucks," "wenches," is that it places a stigma upon an entire class of human beings, numbering millions of people; it fails to recognize personal character and individual merit. However talented or cultivated or refined or sensitive or worthy a man or woman may be, his colored blood dooms him to ignominy, and classifies him with the outcast. There are positions of usefulness and honor which he could creditably fill, to which he cannot aspire by reason of his color. The public sentiment against him, like an untimely frost, destroys even in its germ the noblest aspirations of his soul. Why should he study to become a scholar? Why should he strive after

Some Fruits of Prejudice

intellectual discipline and power? Why should he cultivate the graces? Why should he resist temptation to evil, and seek to show himself noble and Christian, if all his best endeavors are to be met by a sneer? Why should he strive to equal the white man in his virtues if the white man refuses him recognition and denies him the opportunity of utilizing his attainments? The great motive force of human progress is hope, the desire of achievement, and the expectation of reward that comes from earnest and worthy effort. What, then, can be expected of a race from which these rewards are withheld, and from whose breast hope is plucked out?

Along with this discouragement, which is well-nigh fatal to progress, there is on the part **Wounded Sensibilities** of the sensitive and refined a deep sense of injury. The Negro knows that he is not personally responsible for his color; he was not consulted in the choice of his race connections; he cannot remove the obstacles to his progress that his more fortunate white neighbor has put in his way; he is largely helpless, and when he is met by rebuff and insult, and with limitation and restriction, especially when he sees his best endeavors treated with ridicule, and beholds life's most cherished rewards bestowed upon men whom he knows to be his inferiors in everything except color, he feels deeply wounded and oftentimes even almost crushed. He keenly recognizes the injustice of his treatment, and cannot help cherishing in his heart of hearts a feeling of resentment against those who assume to degrade him because of his color. Undoubtedly, in some instances, this feeling of wounded honor, of injustice, of resentment, may take the form of revenge, and he may seek to inflict upon his oppressor the punishment which he honestly feels belongs to one who will wantonly inflict evil upon a fellow human being without cause. It is possible that in many cases among the lower grades of them, crime may be instigated, partly at least, by this feeling of injustice. The Negro feels that he suffers injustice from the white people, and that the only way in which he can avenge himself, or punish wrong, is by himself violating law. As every white man's hand is against him, he feels justified in lifting his hand against the white race. These acts of resentment, of revenge, of crime, resulting from the injuries they suffer by reason of the prejudice against them, react upon the white race and give to them an excuse, at least, for continuing their course of injustice; and thus these two evils act and react, and in some instances utter demoralization in a community results.

If it be asked, "What is the remedy for this unhappy state of things?" the answer is difficult to formulate. If the antipathy results from conscious superiority on the part of the white man and from inherent inferiority on the part of the African, then there is apparently no help for it, unless it be in the exalted magnanimity of the white race, the outgrowth of culture and of the Christian religion, which is willing to recognize, even in the weakness of the Negro, a reason for considerate treatment. "The Ethiopian cannot change his skin," and it is possible that he must always suffer by reason of that fact, so long as he attempts to live on terms of equality under the same flag with the white man. In so far as the prejudice against him results from his ignorance, inferiority, barbarity—the sad heritage of slavery—the only remedy is that which results from education, industry, and

Is There a Remedy?

civilization. His hope is in the spelling-book. When he can establish beyond peradventure that he has the same fundamental qualities of mind, the same possibilities of culture, and when he achieves scholarship and is able to meet the white man on his own ground and contend with him successfully as a laborer and organizer, a thinker, a leader, he will get the recognition that is always accorded to strength.

Those of the rising generation must avail themselves of the opportunities for education now offered to them, and must be satisfied with nothing less than the broadest attainments possible, if they are to wrest from their white associates recognition of their manhood. It is also, doubtless, true that they will be respected, generally, in proportion to their real moral worth. If they are honest, truthful, law-abiding, pure in life, self-restraining, charitable, generous, and just, they will by these high qualities be able, in a certain measure, to enforce from their white neighbors the recognition of the dignity of their character. The transforming power of Christianity will do for them what no other force can possibly accomplish ; just as far as the character of Jesus Christ is illustrated in their lives will they receive from other men the recognition due to those made in the image of God.

History seems to teach that no people ever yet secured a recognition of their rights in their fullness and entirety who were not willing, if need be, to fight for them. Justice sometimes waits on slaughter, and liberty on victory. It would be inexpressibly sad if the conclusion should be forced upon us in this country of liberty and of enlightenment, that the Negro would be compelled to achieve his complete emancipation by force. No one doubts his right to defend his person, his family, and his home against unlawful assault; and it may be that unless he manifests at least a willingness to fight he never can become absolutely free. Let us hope, however, that the inherent justice of his claim to the treatment that belongs to manhood, fortified and emphasized by thrift, industry, and excellence of character, may secure for him without violence that which belongs to him as an American citizen. It should do so in a Christian land.

Violence to be Avoided

Social equality is not a question of law nor of compulsion, but of taste and inclination. The Negro has no right to demand, nor will he himself concede, any claims for social consideration based upon any other than social merits. His political rights, however, he may claim under the Constitution, and the right to earn a living and to have the reward of his labor he may claim under a higher law than the Constitution—the law of immutable right. "Whatsoever a man soweth, that shall he also reap." The time is already approaching when unreasoning prejudice against any class of people will cease to work injustice, and when the political philosophy of equal manhood and the divine teaching of the Fatherhood of God and the brotherhood of man will efface any arbitrary, unreasoning, harmful lines that separate one class of American citizens from another.

One of the most noticeable facts in regard to the relation of the races is the rare patience and self-control thus far exhibited by the Negroes under the most exasperating circumstances. During the days of slavery they were, for the most part, obedient, trustworthy, and faithful; insurrections were almost unheard-of, and acts of revenge unknown. Here and there a slave, more resolute and adventurous than his fellows, escaped

Negro Patience

from slavery and found refuge in the North. During the war, notwithstanding they generally understood that slavery hung in the balance, and that the welfare of the slave was conditioned on the success of the Union arms, most of them remained patiently on the plantations, toiling for their absent masters, who were in the Southern army, fighting to render slavery permanent, and by their tender solicitude for the white women and children entrusted to them, awakened the wonder of the South at their magnanimity and fidelity. They have, in most instances, quietly submitted to the injustice and cruelty of the mobs that have, on mere suspicion of wrong-doing, put hundreds of them to cruel death, and with only a mild protest have allowed themselves to be robbed of their political rights and privileges.

In spite of all obstacles, there has been steady growth of wealth, culture, self-respect, and power among them, and with it has come a growing consciousness of the wrongs they have suffered, and an increasing demand for a recognition of their rights. There is also, if we mistake not, a steady change taking place in the minds of thoughtful

Growth of Public Opinion

white people, North and South, regarding them. Privileges are cheerfully conceded to-day which fifty years ago would have been regarded as impossible. Perhaps it is not too much to predict that public sentiment, which generally moves in right directions, with accelerated ratio, will in another half-century, without violence, concede to them every right and privilege of every kind of which they are deserving.

In this discussion it is worthy of note that the continuance of an unreasoning prejudice against the Negroes will work injury not only to them, but to the white people as well. Slavery was a curse to the master no less than to the slave. No class of people can cherish irrational sentiments toward another without themselves being thereby corrupted. The eight million Negroes of this country, destined to become fifty millions at no distant day, will of necessity exert an influence of increasing potency upon the welfare and progress of the republic. If they are kept down they will drag their oppressors to their own level; if they are permitted to rise, socially, industrially, intellectually, religiously, politically, they will stimulate and help, if not compel, corresponding advancement in all respects on the part of all their white fellow-citizens of even the lowest class. We are a solidarity, and what affects one class must, of necessity, affect all classes. Injustice will work disaster, while justice will promote the public welfare.

VII

THE NEGROES UNDER FREEDOM

THE progress of the Negroes since emancipation is noteworthy. Indeed, it is doubtful whether any race of people has ever accomplished as much along the lines of civilized development in the same period of time. **Progress** While it is true that this progress has not been such as to indicate the possession on their part of any exceptional endowments, it has been sufficient to show that they are possessed of all the ordinary faculties of humanity, and to give great satisfaction to those who have stoutly contended for their essential manhood. Those, however, who are disposed to take an especially optimistic view of the future of the Negroes because of their progress since emancipation, will do well to bear in mind that when this is measured by that of the race with which they come into competition, it is evident that they are not only not overtaking the white people, but that they are, relatively, falling behind. It is probably safe to say that the distance which separates between the average white man of to-day and the average Negro is greater than that which separated them in the days of slavery.

All progress is relative, and in estimating the advance in educational matters, it is a little difficult to form a just judgment based upon the number of those who have been pupils in higher institutions of learning. It is, of course, a matter of congratulation that many thousands of them have been pupils in Negro colleges, universities, and theological seminaries, for a considerable time, where they have received an education far in advance of that possible in former days, and which will be greatly to their advantage in the practical affairs of life. When, however, we come to analyze the facts we find that, for the most part, the grade of instruction in all of these so-called higher institutions has been necessarily of a low order, and that comparatively few have really completed the courses of study. The number of college graduates is, in comparison with the whole number, very small, and that of those who have graduated from a Northern college is

The Negroes Under Freedom

necessarily very much less. It is, therefore, not untrue nor unfair to the Negroes to say that the body of men and women among them who can be said to be well educated is very small indeed. While some of them have taken good rank, even at Harvard and other great institutions, few, if any, either men or women, have achieved any distinction in the line of scholarship. Among the one million six hundred thousand Baptist Negroes, which host includes a very considerable number of those who have had the advantages of more or less education, it is rare to find one who can properly lay claim to any broad attainment, accurate scholarship, or liberal culture. Using the term as it applies to the white race, to include those who have had exceptional advantages from childhood, and who have carried their culture to a high degree, it may be said, without intending to make any invidious comparison, that, strictly speaking, there is to-day among them no educated class. If one were looking for men to fill important professorships in the great universities of the country, he would not expect to find any Negro candidates qualified for the position.

In estimating the value of the Negro public

schools of the South as a factor in their development we should not be misled by familiar terms. Compared with the Northern public schools, those for the Negroes, generally speaking, are very poor, and the results must necessarily correspond with the means used. The masses of the Negro children of to-day are receiving the most primitive sort of education. In order that the public schools may do for them what the public school system of the North is doing for its rising generation, they must have better buildings, better equipment, better teachers, better supervision, indeed, betterment of every kind. "The fountain cannot rise higher than its source," and until the teachers are properly educated for their work it must necessarily be poorly done. There is the most urgent need everywhere in the South for a common sense system of normal training that shall prepare colored men and women, in some measure at least, for the difficult, delicate, important, and urgent work of promoting the moral and intellectual advancement of its rising generation. Until this need is supplied their progress must be slow and unsatisfactory compared with what it might be.

Public School Education

The Negroes Under Freedom

Moreover, the contrast between the denominational schools of the North—academies, colleges, and theological seminaries—and similar institutions for the Negroes is very striking. **Religious Schools** Nowhere in the South, among the Baptists at least, is there a secondary school or academy which can for a moment be compared, for instance, with the Baptist Academy at Worcester, Mass. While the secondary schools are doing valuable work, and are contributing toward the elevation of the race, they are sadly handicapped in equipment and in teaching force. A striking illustration of the existing disparity is found in the fact that while among the less than one million white Baptists of the North there are five strong, well-manned, well-equipped theological seminaries which are every year adding to the number of men thoroughly trained for the work of the pastorate: for the one million six hundred thousand Negro Baptists of the South there is but one theological seminary, poorly equipped, with a small faculty. The lack of properly trained pastors and religious guides is one of the very discouraging features of the situation.

The Negro in America

One of the marked indications of progress is the number of men who are engaged in the editing of newspapers, or in the practice of medicine or law. The care of the sick among eight millions of people is a matter of the highest concern, and their future depends in great degree upon the manner in which this is done. It is frequently said that the race is deteriorating under the new conditions of freedom, and the startling death rate is often cited as confirming this theory. Under the conditions surrounding them since emancipation, they have been peculiarly exposed to the ravages of disease; for ignorance and poverty are great destroyers of human life. The laws of hygiene, of sanitation, and the elements of good housekeeping, as taught in the better schools, are, in some measure at least, mitigating the evils of neglect, and will more and more assist in preventing or checking disease. Those who have been trained as nurses in such schools as Spelman Seminary have become very skillful, and show remarkable adaptation to the delicate and important duties of caring for the sick. Others, educated as pharmacists, exhibit good capacity and find

Editors, Doctors, Lawyers

ready and remunerative employment. The Leonard Medical School at Shaw University, Raleigh, N. C., has a faculty composed of Southern white men of recognized ability and professional standing; their testimony is uniform and emphatic, that the students master the difficult subjects of the course, and that their graduates have no need to blush when they come to take the State examination which admits them to practice on precisely the same terms as white physicians. The number of men who are finding a career for themselves and an opportunity for wide usefulness as physicians is steadily increasing.

While there is a wide-open door for lawyers there are many difficulties, obvious and serious, tending to hinder the rapid increase of those who seek to earn a livelihood by practising law. Enough, however, have overcome these difficulties and established their claim to respectful consideration, to warrant the conclusion that the legal profession will have hereafter an increasing number of Negroes capable of attending to all the ordinary legal interests of their colored clients. This will probably result in securing for them a larger measure of justice in the courts.

As yet they cannot be said to be a reading class. Their poverty and ignorance, as well as their lack of interest in public affairs, are hindrances to the large success of efforts to establish journals upon a paying basis. Their newspapers, as a whole, are small and are issued weekly; they are not published in the best style, and show all the limitations which are incident to a limited circulation, lack of subscribers, and of advertising patronage. With all its shortcomings, no one, however, can dispute the fact that the Negro press has become a power. It affords an opportunity for the race to voice its highest aspirations, to assert as well as to defend itself; and nothing, perhaps, more emphatically marks the transition from the *ante bellum* days of slavery to the period of liberty than the fearless independence and forcefulness of its editorial utterances. Negro editors are at once the proof and the prophecy of Negro progress.

To the question, Is there a professional class among them? I must give a negative reply. As has been seen, there are teachers, preachers, lawyers, doctors, and editors; there are men of good abilities and respectable attainments; but their status as men of learning, re-

The Negroes Under Freedom

sources, and effectiveness, as independent factors in promoting the progress of civilization, is yet to be fixed. Tanner's "Raising of Lazarus," and Paul Dunbar's verses, are prophecies of æsthetic talent.

It is not so easy to measure, or to state with definiteness, the industrial progress made by the Negroes since emancipation. Slavery was a system of enforced labor which developed among them no small degree of industrial skill and practical intelligence as body servants, domestics, coachmen, gardeners, farmers, mechanics, blacksmiths, carpenters, etc. A very considerable number acquired valuable habits, and no small amount of self-directing productive industry. Even in the cotton fields and sugar plantations, and amid the hardest conditions, thousands learned the lesson of steady toil. For the most part, however, such labor was not only compulsory and irksome, but was unaccompanied by thrift, economy, or any of the pleasures that are a part of the daily work of free men.

Industrial Progress

When they were set free, many of them naturally looked back upon labor as a badge of servitude, and confounded their newly acquired freedom with idleness. It could hardly be expected that four million slaves, suddenly liberated from bondage, without capital, without industrial appliances, without experience in self-directed labor, should at once become industrious, economical, thrifty, and efficient. On the whole, however, the transition from slavery to freedom was characterized by less retrogression, idleness, shiftlessness, suffering, and pauperism, than might have been anticipated. As a class they have shown an aptitude for self-support. Their toil, while often both unintelligent and unremunerative, has been remarkably general and constant. Multitudes have acquired homes of their own; they pay taxes upon hundreds of millions of dollars which they have accumulated, and they are to-day, as they ever have been, the chief wealth producers of the South. In the cotton fields and the cane brakes, on the farms, in the laundry and the kitchen, on the railroads, in the mines, and wherever service of a rough and unskilled kind is required, they are found performing it.

There has been a steady tendency toward eliminating them from the realm of skilled labor, and wherever they come into sharp com-

The Negroes Under Freedom

petition with white men they are generally forced to give way. Multitudes of them still find employment, however, as waiters in hotels, as porters on the cars, as cab drivers, and in other occupations requiring more or less intelligence and skill, and it is unquestionably true that their education, with its increase of general intelligence, has improved the quality of their labor of all kinds. This is notably true in the matter of home keeping, although vast improvement is yet possible and desirable. In connection with almost all of the schools of a higher order, there has been more or less attention given to what is called industrial education. Pupils have been required to care for their own rooms, to share in keeping the school buildings in proper order, and in looking after the yard and grounds. Young women have been taught the rudiments of cooking, darning, sewing, dressmaking ; here and there have been printing establishments, where they have been instructed in the "mysterious art"; and occasionally farms have been worked in connection with the school by pupil labor, but not with marked success. There have been attempts made to teach the trades, as at Tuskeegee, Ala., as well as the use of tools in wood and iron work, as at Hampton, Va., and Marshall. Tex. As yet, however, no systematic scheme of industrial training, such as is carried on at the Pratt Institute of Brooklyn, the Drexel Institute of Philadelphia, or the School of Technology in Boston, has been undertaken. Such schools need to be established for them unless they are to be permanently excluded from the higher walks of industry.

The political status of the Negroes is quite anomalous. As slaves they had no political privileges whatever, and, with the single and curious exception that they were reckoned as a factor in determining the number of congressmen to be allotted to the slave-holding States, they were political nonentities—not persons, but property. When liberated from slavery they were, necessarily, wholly without experience in the performance of civic duties, and had no true sense of the responsibilities attaching to citizenship. Not only this, but their long subjection to the absolute dominance of the white man and their entire ignorance regarding political matters, being unable to read, seemed to exclude them from even the possibility of sharing in political privileges. The conferring

Political Status

The Negroes Under Freedom

upon them of the right of suffrage, with all the privileges and responsibilities of citizenship, without any preparation on their part, was an unprecedented, radical, and revolutionary act, full of peril both to themselves and to the republic. Thoughtful men at the North as well as the South stood aghast at the spectacle of giving over the destinies of several Southern States into the hands of a horde of ignorant, degraded, inexperienced, suddenly liberated African slaves. The justice of this drastic measure was stoutly disputed, and its wisdom as an act of statesmanship is still denied by multitudes of thinking men.

It is impossible, in a brief outline, such as is this, to go into the details of this strange experiment, and any general statements that may be made regarding it will doubtless be open to criticism. It is worthy of consideration, however, that after the lapse of a generation, the Negroes of the South, now twice as many as when enfranchised, are still nominally in possession of the ballot, and with no marked public sentiment, either North or South, looking toward depriving them of it. It is true that in some of those States where they greatly outnumber the whites, or where their numbers are such as to make Negro dominance a menace, they are largely deprived of the power that is supposed to attach to majorities; nowhere in the South are they in control. Over against this, however, it should be said that tens of thousands of Negroes throughout the South exercise the right of suffrage freely, and have their votes counted. In many of the States they occupy seats in the legislature, and fill other important public positions. Political freedom is a political school. In no other way than by the exercise of the rights of free men could they have acquired self-consciousness as Americans, and have been stimulated to prepare themselves for the discharge of the duties devolving upon them as the citizens of a free republic. Slowly but surely there is coming to them in its completeness the recognition of their rights as integral factors of the commonwealth, and this is a great gain. The fact of their citizenship, and the conviction that it is irrevocable, is a potent factor in securing for them the benefits of the public schools maintained by the States, and the advantages of the higher schools supported by Christian philanthropy.

Since Frederick Douglass, no Negro of commanding ability has appeared as a political

The Negroes Under Freedom

leader or statesman. Nevertheless, a very considerable number have filled high public offices acceptably, and many have shown an intelligent appreciation of the responsibilities involved in official position.

Perhaps the severest test of their progress in civilization is their social status. They are surrounded on every side by a strong white race, chiefly Anglo-Saxon, accustomed to lordship, proud of its prestige, and with a strong inclination to refuse to recognize the claims of the African to any consideration other than that prompted by pity or general humanity. That this spirit is relaxing, however, and that there is a growing disposition on the part of the white people to recognize the manhood of the Negroes, is evident. The commencement exercises at some of the Negro schools are now attended by white people of high social position, who go, not to gratify their curiosity, least of all to express their contempt, but to indicate their interest, appreciation, and sympathy. At the Ministers' Institutes held in several Southern States, under the direction of Negro superintendents, the ablest white men participate without hesitation as public lecturers. What the

Social Status

final solution of the relation of the races will be does not yet appear, but this much is certain, that manhood, culture, worth of character, and dignity of conduct, will assert themselves and command respect. The Negroes will in the end receive whatever is their due.

The conclusion reached by this re-study of the present status of the eight million Negroes, thirty-five years after emancipation, may be summarized thus:

Summary

1. In almost all the elements of civilization the race, as a whole, has made distinct progress. While the condition of multitudes of them is still deplorable, it is encouraging to note that the degree of illiteracy among them is less than that of the inhabitants of Spain, who have enjoyed centuries of freedom and so-called civilization.

2. The progress of the Negroes has been due to the fact of their relationship to civilized white men; they have shown a capacity to adopt rather than to originate, to follow, rather than to lead, to imitate, rather than to create. Thus far they have shown very little ability to organize and direct, except in local and limited affairs.

The Negroes Under Freedom

3. The supreme test of their capacity to contend with the white man, on equal terms, is yet to come. The struggle for industrial recognition and for political equality promises to be a bitter one, and the Negroes are badly handicapped in entering it.

4. What is needed pre-eminently, to-day, to insure not only the welfare and progress of the Negroes, but the well-being of the States in which they live and the republic in its entirety, are : (1) The strengthening of the great Christian schools established for their benefit by Northern beneficence ; these are their chief hope ; (2) the improvement of the public school system by lengthening the terms, extending the period of attendance, and supplying them with a large increase of well-trained teachers ; (3) the creation of a few well-equipped industrial schools where men can be trained for leadership.

5. There is imminent peril in any scheme which seeks to segregate the Negroes. Their interests are identical with the interests of their white fellow-citizens. Co-operation has in it "the promise and the potency" of great things for the race.

VIII

THE IDEAL AMERICAN REPUBLIC[1]

THERE is a consensus of opinion among intelligent Americans as to the form of government and the character of laws and institutions which are most desirable for us and for our neighbors, for our children, and ultimately for the world. We cherish in common a lofty conception of a free government, in which every citizen is a sovereign, and every sovereign a wise, patriotic, and just man. Our loyalty is philanthropic, and not selfish; zealous without bitterness. "With malice toward none, with charity for all, with love for the right as God gives us to see the right," we earnestly strive for the realization and perpetuation of an ideal republic, whose foundations are truth, and whose blessings are for humanity.

---

[1] The following paper was not prepared originally for this series but is inserted here because of the pertinence of the discussion. The Ideal Republic is based not on race distinction but on manhood. To call this a "white man's government" is a denial of the doctrine of human equality—the basal idea of our civilization.

The Ideal American Republic

We are ruled by our ideals. A thought of purpose clearly conceived is a dominant force in human life. Tell me what the ideals of an individual are, and I will tell you the secret forces and controlling tendencies of his life. The ideals of a people are prophetic of their destiny. The character of the government, or the ideal of the republic which the present generation most strongly cherishes, will very largely determine the final outcome of that momentous experiment of self-government which is now being tried on so large a scale on this continent. We do well, therefore, to examine that ideal with two purposes in view: first, to correct it if it be faulty.

Reasons for this Discussion

The thought of human liberty and aspiration after freedom is as old as the race, and history records no struggles which have been more intense and magnificent than those that have been waged for the attainment of these ends. The difficulties attending the adjustment of the machinery of government so as to secure liberty for the individual and safety and prosperity for the masses, have ever been so many and so great that the record of the efforts to establish free government is largely a record of failures.

Republics have arisen only to fall; great victories in the struggle for freedom have been won only to be followed by disaster and defeat; and freedom has lifted its voice only to be drowned in anarchy and strangled in despotism. Nevertheless, there has been progress running through the centuries, and human freedom is to-day more nearly within the reach of the common people than ever before in the history of the world.

It is perhaps not too much to say that the republic of the United States at the present time more fully conforms to the hopes and aspirations of the lovers of liberty than any government which has ever existed. The ideal of what men desire has become clearer and clearer as time has gone by, and they have made successive and gratifying steps in the advancement toward its complete realization. Much remains to be done, however, before these lofty conceptions shall be fully embodied in law and practice, and it is, perhaps, possible that what men are striving for is not wholly attainable. If we of to-day are cherishing vague and ill-founded hopes, and are trying to establish a government that can exist only in the imagination, that has no counterpart in history, and that must be always deluding and disappointing to us—an *ignis fatuus*—then it is well that we should modify our ideals and moderate our expectations, for an impossible Utopia is not worth striving for. Certainly nothing can be lost by an intelligent, searching discussion of the ideal we cherish of the possible republic. It will make clearer to us our thought; will expose whatever of error may be in it, and will open the way for such modification of our conceptions as logic or fact may necessitate. No true ideal has anything to fear from the most rigid analysis or the most critical examination.

A second reason for the discussion of the ideal republic is that it affords an opportunity to discern the hindrances or dangers that may lie in the way of its complete realization. No great truth relating to human well-being ever yet embodied itself in institutions without opposition. The history of liberty is a history of struggle, of conflict, of carnage, of resistance, of victory, of defeat; triumph over difficulties; progress in spite of enemies; success purchased at enormous cost. "Eternal vigilance is the price of liberty."

When we scrutinize our ideal of the republic as it ought to be and contrast that ideal with the state of things that actually exists around us, we shall be spurred to increased zeal in behalf of all agencies that promise real help in bringing facts into harmony with theory. It should kindle our enthusiasm for liberty.

When we set over against this ideal the medieval, despotic theory of a State that still finds among us so many adherents, we shall be startled at the contrast and awakened to the perils that beset us. Light has no fellowship with darkness. Liberty and despotism are implacable foes.

Our Possible Destiny

Standing as we do, looking back over more than a century, tracing the progress that we have already made, taking a survey of the present condition of affairs and of our relations to the future, we are able, without the assumption of any extraordinary powers, to forecast the time—not far removed, as we reckon historic periods—when the United States may embrace even a much larger territory than that already comprised within its magnificent limits; when its population will be numbered by the hundreds of millions; when its wealth will be fabulous and its commerce enormous; and when its influence upon the world will far sur-

The Ideal American Republic

pass that ever exerted by any other nation. All the signs of the times and the teachings of history clearly indicate the almost limitless possibilities in the development of the internal power and the worldwide influence of this republic.[1]

The ideal which many have set before themselves who to-day are engaged in the active work of molding public opinion, of shaping the character of our institutions, of determining our destiny, is no narrow one. It is as broad as human liberty, as comprehensive as the varied human interests concerned, and as far-reaching as our influence may ever extend. It can make very little difference to those of the present generation who are now actively engaged in the responsibilities and cares of life, what conception of the republic may ultimately obtain in the popular mind, and find expression in law and in institutions, because in our time no radical changes are likely, even if they are possible. Our liberties are secure. It does concern future generations, however, whether the institutions that we are now es-

---

[1] This was written before the late Spanish war gave us Porto Rico directly and indirectly Hawaii. Will Cuba and the Philippine Islands come next?

tablishing, the laws that we are enacting, the philosophy that we are inculcating, the spirit that we are engendering, are to be consonant with the highest ideal of liberty and progress, or whether they are such as to bring about a curtailment of their liberty or an abridgment of their highest happiness.

Our thinking of to-day is for the future ; our discussions are for the benefit of unborn generations, and our contention is for an ideal that concerns the race. We are striving to establish American institutions whose beneficent privileges shall be enjoyed by successive generations for a thousand years to come. In the future, those who are living in the full exercise of whatever privileges or opportunities are then afforded, will regard those of the present time who are helping to determine the nature of our institutions either with gratitude for the blessings they enjoy, or with feelings of bitterness or contempt—if we fail to transmit to them these free institutions unimpaired.

Building for the Future

What, then, are those fundamental conceptions which underlie our experiment of self-government, and which we believe ought to

The Ideal American Republic

give character to our nation and its institutions? What, in broad outline, is the Ideal Republic?

The first element is the sovereignty of the people. The fundamental truth is that the government derives its powers from the consent of the governed. The people are sovereigns. A republic is self-governed. It "is a government of the people, for the people, and by the people." It is the assertion of the radical doctrine of the inherent right of the people to govern themselves. There is here a denial of the fiction of the "divine right of kings." Government is simply an expression of the will of the governed; and those who, for the time being, exercise rule or authority, do it, not by virtue of their own right, nor by the law of inheritance, nor by divine appointment, but because of the simple fact that they have been chosen by the free suffrages of the people as their representatives or rulers to exercise the power temporarily delegated to them for the benefit of those who confer it. The people who elect rulers to-day can, in accordance with the terms of the Constitution which they themselves prescribe, elect another set to-morrow to take their places and to exercise

Source of Power

full authority during their term of office. According to this conception, there can be no such thing as royalty or aristocracy, and consequently, no such broad distinction between the people and their rulers as necessarily obtains in monarchical, aristocratical, or hierarchical governments. The people are kings and rulers; their will is law. The proud monarch proclaims himself the State; the highest officials in a republic are the servants of the people. We, the people, ordain constitutions, make legislatures, establish courts, create judges, elect governors, constitute armies, levy taxes, regulate and execute laws. We sit on juries, and are entitled to trial by our peers. Our liberties are in our own keeping, our rights are inviolate, our homes are our castles. We call no man lord, because we ourselves are the sources of power. The great chasm between the government and the people, as two separate forces with distinct and conflicting interests, is filled up and sodded over. The people are themselves the government. There can be, according to this idea, no privileged classes, no haughty monarchs, no blue-blood aristocrats, no titled nobility, no arrogant hierarchy: no distinctions based on race or color.

The Ideal American Republic

Growing out of this fundamental conception, and necessarily connected with it, is the doctrine of equal rights. The ringing words of the Declaration of Independence that "all men are created equal," sweep away at one stroke all class distinctions and recognize the far-reaching principle that in the eye of the law, as members of the commonwealth, the rights of one man are just as sacred as those of another. However men may differ in intellectual endowments, in moral character, in possessions, color, or social position, politically they are equal. The vote of one man has the same weight as that of another man; the vote of the laborer goes just as far as that of the capitalist in fixing the character of the government under which he lives and in determining the persons who are to exercise authority. This truth blots out at once all distinctions growing out of race, color, or condition, and lays broad, deep, enduring foundations in the doctrine of the essential dignity of human nature. Whatever artificial or incidental conditions may separate men socially or financially, "a man's a man for a' that." This recognition of the inherent dignity of the soul, this

Human Equality

radical doctrine of human equality, this emphatic declaration of the right of each and every man to his own life, liberty, and pursuit of happiness, as embodied in the fundamental charter which underlies our political superstructure, marks a tremendous advance in the progressive civilization of the race.

This great doctrine of human equality furnishes the basis of a true socialism. The consciousness among the toiling masses of their own inherent worth as men, and the deep-seated aspirations cherished by many of them for better conditions, underlies much of the unrest of our times, and is slowly but surely working out great revolutions in social relations, industrial conditions, and political institutions. We are rapidly passing through successive stages of a mighty change, and are tending toward a form of socialism that has in it the "promise and potency" of a vast amelioration of economic evils, social inequalities, and political disabilities. Equal rights is a mighty solvent of the problems of discontent.

<small>A True Socialism</small>

Another way of stating the doctrine of equal rights, is to say that our Republic rests upon individualism. The individual is the political

The Ideal American Republic

unit. Each man stands or falls for himself. It does not matter, so far as the conception of his rights is concerned, whether he is wise or ignorant, strong or weak, rich or poor, white, black, or red, he stands for what he is—an individual, a personality whose rights and privileges are as dear to him as are those of any other person in the world. For political purposes he stands alone; his personality is inviolate; his rights are sacred. Within his own domain he is an autocrat. The emperor upon his throne is not more complete in himself than the humblest voter in a republic. The individual is endowed with all the essential attributes of humanity. He has intellect, conscience, and will. He is himself an epitome of man. Whatever concerns humanity concerns him; whatever affects human rights affects his rights; whatever enhances human dignity enhances his dignity. Whatever limits, dwarfs, or hinders the race, equally and in the same manner, *ceteris paribus*, affects him; whatever principles of justice apply to the masses of people apply to him individually. Politically he calls no man master; acknowledges no authority greater than his own. He

Individualism

recognizes no caste from which he is rightfully excluded, no class that has rights or privileges that he cannot aspire to; and he submits to no limitations of his liberty that are not necessitated by consideration for the liberties and rights of his fellow-men.

Man, created in the image of his Maker, is complete in himself. He is a free moral agent, capable of choice and competent for self-government. He is responsible directly to God for his conduct and character, and no man can stand between him and the judgment to come; he must appear for himself before his Maker and "give an account of the deeds done in the body." No human daysman can interpose as advocate; he must bear his own burden. This is the plain teaching of Scripture, that sets forth man's autonomy as a moral being and his responsibility as a free agent.

The Dignity of Human Nature

Our theory of government gives to man politically the same status that the Bible gives to him morally and religiously. He is a political entity; an independent citizen; must act as an individual, and bear the responsibility of those actions. He is entitled to that freedom which ensures him the fullest unfolding of all his powers, the largest exercise possible of all his normal activities, the greatest practicable enjoyment of the pleasures he most desires, and the widest career that is compatible with his relations to his fellow-men. Then the responsibility for his action must rest with himself. If he makes mistakes he must suffer the consequences. If he will not work neither shall he eat. If he violates law or interferes with the rights of his neighbor he must suffer punishment. No plea of ignorance will avail him. He cannot hide behind any society, or screen himself by any plea of coercion or oath of obedience. He is a subject of the Republic, a citizen of the nation which has enfranchised and ennobled him. Each American voter walks erect among his fellow-citizens, the peer of the noblest and the equal of the highest.

As one of the sovereign people, the source of political power, a constituent member of the body politic for which all power and all authority is exercised, an integral element of government itself, he not only has all the rights that pertain to the most favored private citizen, but he himself may aspire to the highest office; a sovereign *de jure*, he may be-

The Man Greater Than the Office

come a sovereign *de facto*, by the free suffrage of his fellow-citizens. Aspiration after high political honors and power is entirely consonant with his position as an equal member of the Republic. This doctrine confers upon him the highest dignity. His simple manhood is his title to respect. Exalted ability or exceptional attainment—by virtue of which he may be elected to office—enables him to confer dignity upon the place which he is called to fill, if he fills his office with ability and fidelity, and when he lays aside the temporary authority with which he may be clothed, he loses none of his dignity, but returns to private life with the consciousness that the man is greater than the office.

If there is any institution upon which rests the special divine favor, it is the family. God has constituted the home as the sphere in which is to be developed many of the sweetest graces of womanhood and strongest virtues of manhood. The relation of husband and wife, of parents and children, of brother and sister, are peculiarly tender and strong. It is in the family that children are to learn to be affectionate, patient, helpful, respectful to

The Autonomy of the Family

The Ideal American Republic

age, tender to helplessness, obedient to authority, and reverent toward God. The father is the founder of the family, the head of the household, the priest of the home circle. The mother is the helpmeet for him. Within the sphere of the home they should be supreme. No external power should obtrude itself into its sacred precincts. The parents, as long as they are competent and willing to discharge aright their parental obligations, should be left free to follow their own choice as to the education and training of their children.

The doctrine of individualism recognizes the inestimable value to the individual of association with his fellows. Man never reaches his highest development intellectually or religiously, or achieves his greatest successes, apart from society. **Value of Society** The anchorite is doomed to failure. Monasticism is a perversion of life. Men need the attrition that comes from active association with other men in business; each sex needs the constant influence of the other. The art of living together is one of man's noblest achievements. Sociology is a science second in importance only to theology. The great thing to be insisted upon is that society shall be free to form and reform on planes of ascending development.

But these facts in no wise militate against the great truth here stated, that the relation between the citizen and the Republic is a personal, individual relation. He is recognized by the government under which he lives as a man, capable of performing a man's duties, and of exercising a man's privileges. It confers upon him the dignity of citizenship, and it has a right to his personal loyalty. Individualism bestows honor and imposes obligations.

Whatever subordinate relations he sustains to his family, his associates, or to society, his prime allegiance is to the Republic. He is first of all an American. He hoists no other flag above the Stars and Stripes.

Man was born for freedom; his highest intellectual and spiritual development, indeed, the perfection of his manhood, is dependent essentially upon his liberty. He should, as far as practicable, be free from all external restraints. His actions should be self-originated, self-controlled, and should be unrestricted just as far as the circumstances by which he is surrounded will admit. One of his

The Birthright of Freedom

characteristics as an individual, a personality, a moral being, is freedom in choosing his own vocation, determining his own activities, selecting his own companions, deciding upon his own home, educating his own children, settling his own creed, and electing his own rulers. In as far as he is restricted in his liberty he is robbed of his birthright; and in as far as he weakly and voluntarily surrenders his own freedom to another he emasculates himself.

Liberty is not license. Freedom is conduct self-regulated in conformity with reason and the eternal verities of the universe. Only a moral being can be free, and morality implies responsibility.

Of course, when men live in communities there must be restriction by government— some rule of action that shall preserve the rights of the community on the one hand and the rights of the individual on the other. Men living together can no more dispense with government than they can dispense with air; it is a condition of society. The necessity of some regulative power, of some restrictive agency, of some authoritative execution of punishment for wrong-doing, grows out

Government a Necessity

of man's ignorance, selfishness, and other natural limitations. Anarchy, which rebels against all law and denies the necessity of any government, is wholly irrational, ignoring as it does the essential nature of man and the plainest teachings of history. In its revolt against the cruelty of despotism it swings to the opposite extreme of no government, and for the oppression of the tyrant or the misrule of the legal authorities it would substitute the savage fury of the mob. Because governments are imperfect it would utterly abolish them. It would destroy the sun to get rid of the spots on its surface. Mobs are symptoms of political rottenness. Anarchists are the haters of government and the enemies of freedom.

Men have an unbounded right to combine for just purposes and to use righteous means to obtain them. Trades unions, labor organizations, combinations of capitalists, are praiseworthy, as long as permeated by justice. But the individual laborer—mechanic, business man, or capitalist—has the right of liberty in disposing of his labor, his skill, or his capital. When trusts ruthlessly crush out the small capitalist, and labor unions resort to violence to prevent individuals working to earn bread for their families, they do violence to the great doctrine of individualism.

Government, however, does not exist for its own sake; its only *raison d'être* being its utility as an agency for the advancement of the common welfare and the promotion of individual prosperity. **Government a Means, Not an End** If all men were wise, moral, and strong, there certainly would be need of less government than there is now; but as long as they are ignorant, selfish, and weak, there will continue to be, for their own sakes, as well as for the good of the community, the necessity of a central power of regulation. Just as soon, however, as this central power arrogates to itself undue importance, or seeks self-aggrandizement at the expense of the people, it becomes an impertinence and an evil to be remedied or removed.

Returning to the idea of liberty, let us ask, What is meant by liberty? What are the elements that enter into the conception of human freedom? **Liberty Analyzed**

Free Thought. The first, most obviously, is freedom of thought. Man is an intellectual being and every normal individual possesses all that is necessary to constitute him an independent thinker. He is endowed with powers of observation, self-consciousness, memory, imagination, logical faculties, and is able to observe, analyze, compare, and decide for himself all the ordinary questions that present themselves to his mind and call for judgment as the basis of action.

Of course he is limited by the ineradicable distinctions between truth and error which he cannot, by any process of thought, change. The axioms of mathematics, the laws of physics, and the established rules of philosophy, are not the products of the human mind, but of the divine mind; and a man in his thinking is necessarily limited by the laws of thought and the facts of creation. Within these limits, however, he should have great freedom; indeed, there can be no thinking, properly so called, which is not free. The acceptance of propositions formulated by others does not necessarily imply thinking. Faith, in so far as it is merely an assent to an intellectual dogma, or the acceptance of the result of another's thinking, without an understanding of its processes, is not an attribute of freedom. To think is to bring one's self into immediate contact with facts and truths, and to see for one's self the relations that facts and thoughts sustain to each other and that premises sustain to conclusions. Free thought is one of our most precious privileges, and any limitations laid upon its exercise is a curbing of our liberty, an abridgment of our manhood, a species of enslavement. No man is free who is forced to blindly accept the conclusions of another man's reasoning. Every free man creates his own creed.

The Historic Spirit. I, of course, recognize the fact that any intelligent thinker will be helped by other men's thinking, and that all progress in thought, whether in the line of science, philosophy, or religion, is immensely aided by a genuine historic spirit, and that no one who seeks a firm foundation in great questions can afford to ignore the work already done in the line of his investigations by the great minds that have preceded him. No man, with any safety, can break violently, suddenly, or capriciously with the past. Nevertheless, every individual, in as far as his capacities will allow and his circumstances will admit, should, before adopting them as his own, re-think the thoughts of other men, examine the relations of their conclusions to their premises, and decide for himself as to the soundness of their reasonings. In other words, every man should put the stamp of his own originality on every article of his belief; but whether he can do this, or is willing to do it, the great and undeniable truth—the truth for which I most earnestly contend—remains, that he should be free to do so. Freedom of thought is his inalienable right, and is that for which he should battle as for his life.

If it should be said that men are incapable of thinking for themselves, and must therefore accept the formulas elaborated for them by authority, I answer that such creeds have about the same value for them that a sword has for a man without hands.

If it be said that men who attempt to think for themselves may fall into error and be led astray, I reply, that to profess to believe what one does not understand, and to accept a creed as an act of obedience, is to *be* very far astray and involved in most hurtful error. Nothing could be more irrational than to assert that "we believe a thing because it is absurd." This is to make a denial of the trustworthiness of our mental processes, the basis of our highest mental attainments. We declare ourselves fools in order that we may be accounted wise.

A Free Bible. Recognizing as I do the incomparable place occupied by the sacred Scriptures as the inspired word of God, given for man's spiritual illumination, I lay special stress upon the right of every man to read that great book for himself. The Bible should be free. The right of private interpretation should be sacred. No other book ever wrought so powerfully for the enfranchisement of the race as has the Bible. No people can be permanently enslaved who are familiar with its pages and animated by its spirit. The Bible is the great charter of human liberty. The enemies of freedom hate the Bible. The progress of soul liberty received a vast impulse when Wycliffe, Luther, and others gave it to the common people, translating it into their mother tongue.

Free Speech. Closely connected with freedom of thought is freedom of speech; for it is just as necessary for a man to give utterance to his thought as it is for him to think it; indeed, thought in any wide, true sense, is practically impossible without communication with other minds. It is of little avail to me that I am untrammeled in thought, if I may not bring myself, by means of my thinking, into soul relationship with my fellow-beings. If I have arrived at some great truth, it is my privilege, if not my duty, to communicate the truth to those about me. If I am in doubt as to my own processes or acts, the results of my own observations and reasoning, it is my right to confer with those about me, either privately or publicly, and to seek, by their assistance, to test my conclusions, the validity of my thought, or by their aid to modify my views.

Limits of Free Speech. Of course there are practical limitations to the freedom of speech. The State should protect the reputation of its subjects, and it must preserve its own existence. Mobs are intolerable, and speeches that incite to riot and murder justly subject the speakers to the danger of arrest and punishment as disturbers of the peace. There must be due vigilance in the maintenance of public order, but it may and should be used without any infringement of true freedom of speech. Government, generally, is perhaps more liable to err on the side of severity than on that of laxity. The blasphemies of infidels, the tirades of sandlot orators, and the wild utterances of anarchists, are less to be dreaded than is the brutal force of a czar suppressing free speech.

Freedom of speech for men who are necessarily limited in their powers, and are feeling their way toward wise conclusions, is essential for the common progress of the race in its pursuit after truth. Without free speech intellectual progress would be confined largely to individuals ; by means of it the conclusions reached by the few become the possession of the many, and the progress of the one great thinker becomes the stimulus for the advancement of the multitude.

Unnecessary rigor in suppressing open-air meetings, violence used to punish or intimidate men from speaking the truth, are crimes against liberty. Any institution or cause that cannot endure the light of the nineteenth century should retire to the darkness of the fifteenth.

Freedom of debate is not a meaningless phrase to juggle with. It is a great weapon for exposing error, refuting falsehood, removing prejudice, uncovering fallacies, establishing truth, and awakening enthusiasm for it.

A Free Press. Closely allied to freedom of speech, and, indeed, separable from it only by an arbitrary line of distinction, is the liberty of the press. If I have a right to utter my thoughts privately to others, or in public discussion or discourse, I have the right to print them in the columns of newspaper, tract, magazine, or book. Libraries are the great storehouses of thought which register the achievements of individuals and of the race. They are among the mightiest monuments of human greatness, and are the most valuable treasures handed down by one generation to another. They are the milestones marking the advance of the race in its search after truth; the *foci* in which are collected the great lights of all places and of all ages; the fountains to which each succeeding generation goes to drink from the treasured store gathered for them in the centuries past. They are the centers of ever-widening, radiating influence; the indispensable aids to progress; and to interpose any obstacle in the way of making books is to throw obstruction in the upward pathway of the race. An *index expurgatorius* is a shackle upon the development of civilization. No man is as wise as all men; no party knows as much as all parties; no ancient ever stood on the same high level as the moderns. This age is wiser than all preceding ages; the men of to-day are better prepared to sit in judgment on any question of interest to human thought than the men of any other generation. Those that come after us will be wiser than we are. To attempt to hinder the advancement of thought by limiting the liberty of the press is an attempt to fly in the face of God himself. He created man in his own image; implanted within him an insatiable thirst for knowledge; inspired him with an irrepressible desire not only to know and to think, but also to communicate his thought, and to put it into permanent shape for the benefit of future generations.

It hardly needs to be added that the freedom of the press, the unrestricted right to make books that contain discussions of all kinds of questions—political, philosophical, scientific, social, theological—does not imply that men are at liberty to make and circulate immoral literature for the corruption of the young, but it does remove the ban from books that may be regarded as false in doctrine or unsound in teaching.

The freedom of the press, so characteristic of our country to-day, is one of the safeguards of liberty and one of the strongest aids in our progress. The great secular dailies and religious weeklies stimulate intellectual activity, foster intelligence, and assist in creating a sound public opinion on all the vital questions of the hour.

Whenever the press is palsied by the touch of intolerance or of fear it loses its freedom, its power, its usefulness. A muzzled press in a free country is an anachronism.

Liberty of Conscience. Not less important than either of the elements mentioned is freedom of conscience. Every moral creature must determine his own activity; an activity controlled from without ceases to be moral. When we perform an action under restraint it is not our own action; we are no longer free men, but slaves. In its final analysis every moral action rests upon the deliverance of conscience, and freedom is simply the power that I have to act in accordance with that deliverance. If I do that which it condemns I wrong my own nature, do violence to the fundamental conception of freedom, and recognize myself as no longer a moral being, but an immoral one, doing slavishly the behests of another. No act of mine and no line of conduct can be of any avail to me, except it be the outgrowth of my own conviction of its righteousness.

The Ideal American Republic

Freedom of Worship. The people of the United States, in amending the Constitution so as to prohibit the establishment of religion by the government, took a great stride forward in securing the establishment of soul liberty—the essence of all freedom. Any governmental infringement of the right of the individual to worship God according to the dictates of his own conscience is an invasion of the very citadel of his manhood.

Worship of the Almighty God is a spiritual act, not a formal one ; consists in right attitudes of the heart, and not in genuflections of the body. It expresses the relationship **Spirituality of Worship** that the individual sustains directly and immediately with his Maker, and there can, by no possibility, be any intermediary. The moment the so-called act of worship is controlled by a third person, or influenced by any object, it ceases to be worship and becomes form. Man as a spiritual being is closely allied to the Spirit that made him, and finds his highest privilege in spiritual relationship with his Father in heaven. Nothing can take the place of personal communion between the spiritual man and the Divine Spirit. The act of worship, in order to be genuine, must be free; for when it ceases to be free it ceases to be worship. Unless it is spontaneous and correctly represents the man's individual religious experience, his own deep-seated convictions, hopes, and aspirations, it loses its significance. "God is a spirit, and they that worship him must worship him in spirit and in truth."

God only can forgive sins. Forgiveness is the prerogative of Deity—the moral judge of the universe. God alone is the one in whom inheres divine attributes. He only is worthy to be adored. He only can hear prayer. He only can answer prayer—he that hath made us and redeemed us, who feeds, clothes, and sustains us, "in whom we live, move, and have our being." The only true God is to be feared and worshiped. I must worship him for myself. I must make my confession to him; pay my vows to him and him only.

The right to do this, according to the dictates of his own conscience, is one of the most sacred prerogatives of man, and the abridgment of that right is an irreparable injury. Whatever tends to mar the reality of worship, or to substitute for the spontaneous spiritual outgoing of the individual the lifeless form prescribed by another, to which he conforms by stress, is a violent interference with his inestimable privilege of coming directly, personally, sincerely, into religious relationship with his Maker.

Liberty of Action. In speaking of freedom of thought, of speech, of the press, of conscience, of worship, I have necessarily confined myself to man's inner self. Soul liberty, however, is incomplete if it is not supplemented by civil liberty. Man should not only be free to think, but free to act; his "pursuit of happiness" is necessarily conditioned by his tastes, and he himself must be his own judge of what will best contribute to that happiness. Some men find it in exploring wildernesses, in searching for the North Pole, in traversing unknown seas, in sounding the depths of the ocean, in studying the habits of the wild beasts of the forest; some men find it in mercantile pursuits, in the accumulation of wealth; some in the development of great industries, or the building of railroads; some in philosophic pursuits, others in missionary enterprises. It is evident that the happiness of the individual and of the race is conditioned upon freedom in its pursuit. Pursuit of happiness is happiness.

Of course men are to be restrained in their liberty of action when such liberty leads them unwisely or unjustly to do that which interferes with the happiness or prosperity of their neighbors or is clearly inconsistent with the general welfare. Government has a right to interpose to prevent individuals from doing those things which are hurtful to the community, and, undoubtedly, in rare instances, it has a right to interpose in behalf of the individual himself, to restrain him from doing that which will be manifestly to his own detriment—this, however, only on the supposition that he is incompetent to govern himself. The welfare of the individual, as well as of society, requires the freedom of the individual in his own line of activity, and it is better for society and better for the individual, even if in the exercise of his freedom of choice he prefers a line of conduct that may bring him disaster and disappointment instead of success. The government has a right to establish asylums for the confinement of the insane and prisons for the punishment of the vicious; and it may lay its restraining hand upon the individual to prevent him from following a line of conduct which in its example is clearly harmful to the young and thus detrimental to the public weal. Nevertheless, the great, general truth remains that the individual should be free to select his own vocation, to follow his own chosen line of pursuit, to transact business in his own way, to be in all essential particulars a free man.

In a republic based upon the popular will and recognizing the equality of the subject and the freedom of the individual, the ballot is the symbol of liberty. To vote is a high privilege and an unquestionable duty. It is the right of a ruler to rule, and any interference with his right is a just cause for war. It is the duty of a ruler to exercise authority, to execute the functions of his office, and failure to do this is justly condemnable. The voter in the United States is a ruler; he expresses his authority in the ballot; it is his right to express it without restraint; any attempt to lay restrictions upon the freedom of his vote is to deprive him of his authority. In a republic resting upon popular suffrage an attempt to interfere with the free exercise of the suffrage is a blow at the very foundation of the republic itself. To substitute force for freedom at the ballot-box is revolution. To interpose undue

Freedom of the Ballot

authority so as to control against their will the action of voters, is anarchy. It is a crime against the republic, and threatens the existence of government. Freedom of the ballot is the very essence of republicanism. Inasmuch as it is the symbol of authority, its use should be hedged about with proper safeguards. The law should protect the voter from constraint in the casting of his ballot ; should punish bribery or intimidation ; should restrict suffrage to those who have been long enough in the country to become Americanized ; should require some educational qualification ; and should disfranchise confirmed criminals.

The function of the State is the preservation of social order—the protection of the individual in his rights of personal property and reputation. It has nothing whatever to do with determining his religious duties further than to afford him protection in the exercise of his religious privileges. The State should, therefore, be free to perform its functions without ecclesiastical let or hindrance. Grounded, as it is, in the constitution of human nature, it is as clearly divine as the church itself. Indeed, in one sense it may be said that it antedates the

A Free State

church, as a prior expression of the divine will. Its functions are sacred. The high office that it fulfills is the promotion of the well-being of the race. In its relation to its subjects it must be impartial. This cannot be if it lends itself to any sect or branch of the Christian church and attempts to use its vast power as an agency for the propagation of any form of religious belief. As soon as it enters on work of this kind it not only departs from its legitimate sphere of action, but it loses its essential character as a civil institution; it abdicates its own freedom, and by subordinating itself to the church, becomes the servant of the church. It is no longer free, it is bound; it is no longer impartial, it is partisan; it is no longer a judge, it is an advocate; it no longer sustains to the whole of its people the relation of friend and protector, but it becomes, to a portion of them, at least, a possible enemy. Its acts of legislation and administration cease to be free, determined only by considerations of the common welfare, and become narrow, bound, restricted, misdirected, harmful. A free State is a State untrammeled by ecclesiastical chains, unhampered by religious functions, unhindered by sectarian considerations.

I recognize the supreme importance that attaches to genuine religion. Christianity, while it concerns the individual in his relation to his Maker, has at the same time a profound influence in determining his relations to the government under which he lives and to the fellow-citizens among whom he resides. An irreligious man may be a patriot, but he cannot be in the highest sense of the word a good citizen. The obligations of men to deal justly and to respect the rights of their fellow-men, are moral obligations, resting ultimately upon religion, and are determined in their practical working largely by religious convictions. It is hardly conceivable that a republic such as ours could long continue to exist even, much less to perform its high functions as the conservator of popular liberty and the promoter of public weal, if it were thoroughly irreligious. "Only the school bell and the church bell can prolong the echoes of the liberty bell." The restraining force of reverence for God, and the fear of judgment, the sacredness of the oath, the enormity of perjury, the necessity of truthfulness, the binding nature of obligations and contracts, the inviolability of justice, the potency of love for

A Free Church

our neighbors, and the strength of the Golden Rule as a practical guide in the affairs of men, are as enduring as truth itself. These all find their highest sanction in the Christian religion.

The Christian church, while primarily designed for the development of the moral and religious nature and for the rectifying and purifying of the relations between man and his Maker, and while serving as an agency and means for promoting the true worship of Almighty God, has, nevertheless, vital relation to the welfare and the perpetuity of the Republic. It can accomplish its work as an aid to the State far more effectively when left free from any interference, so that it may embody in its life the great principles of its founder.

The State should let the church alone. It need hardly be said that the church, being a religious institution, having to do with religious doctrines and religious practices, and being confined chiefly to the relations between its members and their God, cannot accomplish its work and fulfill its mission in any other way than by freedom. The moment an external power attempts to influence it in its doctrines, its life, its polity, it becomes dwarfed and warped. For a political body, such as a State, composed necessarily of large masses of men who are not in sympathy with the church, who have no proper understanding of its functions, no intelligent knowledge of its doctrines, no appreciation of its life, to undertake to control the church, to legislate for it, to direct its activities, and influence its life, is irrational. It is setting men to the performance of duties for which they are totally unqualified. It is like children playing with edged tools. The history of the Christian church is conclusive in favor of the idea of a church wholly free from civil control and from political alliances.

The idea of the complete separation of Church and State has been one of the great forces that have worked in our history to the advantage of both the State and the Church. His advocacy of this great truth, and the practical embodiment of it in the State which he founded, has given to Roger Williams a place among the world's great thinkers, benefactors, and legislators. Although our progress toward the full realization of this idea has been slow and tedious, the popular mind is at length becoming thoroughly imbued with its soundness.

Roger Williams

I come now to speak of that prime condition

of liberty, free education. If the sketch which I have here set forth of the fundamental conceptions that enter into the ideal of the republic commonly held is a correct one, it at once becomes apparent why there should be a strong insistence upon the necessity of free popular education. In a government by the people each individual voter has entrusted to him the final arbitrament of all national questions, the destiny of the republic. Upon his individual vote may hinge the constitution of legislatures, the character of legislation, the policy of the State, the organization of the Congress of the United States, and possibly the fiscal and economical policy of the entire government. It is safe to say that never before in the history of the world has so much been left to the decision of the common people; never have such momentous issues rested upon the ballot of the individual voter. The safety of the State and all that is involved in it hangs suspended upon the vote of the merest tyro that presents himself for the first time at the polls. The self-preservation of the State, therefore, requires that provision shall be made for the proper education of those into whose hands such great issues are to be placed. Its only safety is in popular education, and by no other means yet devised, except public schools, has the education of the masses of the people been attempted or possible. The free school is indispensable to the free State.

If it be true that the citizen of the United States is to be a free man; free in his own conscience, his own thought, in his expression, in his action, independent of all extraneous and impertinent authorities; free to investigate for himself, to form his own conclusions, and to act upon his convictions, it follows that there must be provided for him some system of training that shall call into fullest exercise all those powers of mind which are essential to this freedom. Such a system has been provided in the public schools, where the course of study is designed to make the pupils acquainted with the rudiments of an education, to put them into possession of their powers of mind, accustom them to sound thinking and to independent utterance, while at the same time so developing moral conceptions and awakening active consciences as to prepare them for the career of freedom that opens before them. The free school is the buttress of our liberties, the bul-

The Ideal American Republic

wark against the waves of ignorance and vice that surge continually against the State. It is the nursery of manhood and womanhood; the training-place of citizenship; the home of independence. Out of it springs excellence of character and preparation for civic duty. To destroy the free school is to strike a deadly blow at the very roots of the tree of liberty. No system of private or parochial schools can compare with the public schools as an agency of universal education.

Résumé

This, then, is my conception of the ideal republic. It contains nothing new, nothing revolutionary, but is simply a restatement of what is in the minds of thousands of earnest thinkers and zealous patriots of the present day. It is the goal toward which human history for centuries past seems to have been slowly tending. It has been more or less completely grasped by the great thinkers of the past, and has consciously or unconsciously swayed the minds and activities of multitudes of those who have thought and fought and wrought for its attainment since the landing of the Pilgrims at Plymouth. The sublime ideal of a free Church within a free State; of a republic of free men;

of a government having for its sole function the promotion of the welfare of its subjects; of a community of intelligent free men dwelling in peace together, untrammeled by needless restrictions, each man free to follow his own inclinations, work out his own destiny, achieve his own success; at the same time the individuals uniting to promote the public weal, to secure general prosperity, and to enable, if possible, all classes to share equally in the beneficent results of a higher, purer civilization than any yet known in human history, has been one of the great factors that has made us what we are to-day, one of the strongest, richest, wisest, and most progressive of nations. It has kindled the eloquence of our orators, guided the pens of our authors, stimulated the researches and labors of our statesmen, illuminated the pages of our poets, aroused the enthusiasm of our generals, given courage and heroism to our patriot armies. It has nerved the arms of the sturdy toilers in our fields, shops, and mines; kindled the ambition of the youth in our schools; and has thrown a halo of beauty around our homes. It has been the beacon light burning upon our shores, seen by all the nations of the earth, alluring to our land

The Ideal American Republic

as to an asylum the vast millions who have fled from the despotism of the old world to the freedom of the new.

The flag of the Republic is to-day a symbol of liberty the world over. It represents the priceless toil and struggle of the past, the unexampled power and splendor of to-day; and it stands for the achievements and glories more resplendent in the future. We of to-day are charged with the sublime duty and entrusted with the lofty privilege of defending this ideal, of guarding our country from encroachments from any source whatever that would seek to take from it any one of the elements of its glory and its strength. The Republic which we have received from our fathers, rich in the legacy of heroic history; the Republic under which we live, whose freedom makes life sweet and rich; the Republic of the future, modified and changed only in as far as may be necessary to embody in fact more absolutely the essential elements that enter into its constitution; the ideal American Republic is ours to establish, cherish, love, protect, and hand down to the generations yet to be. *Esto Perpetua.*

www.ingramcontent.com/pod-product-compliance
Lightning Source LLC
Chambersburg PA
CBHW020921230426
43666CB00008B/1526